PRESERVED
Condiments

VOLUME 1

PRESERVED

Condiments

DARRA GOLDSTEIN / CORTNEY BURNS / RICHARD MARTIN

PHOTOGRAPHY BY DAVID MALOSH

Hardie Grant

NORTH AMERICA

CONTENTS

RECIPES

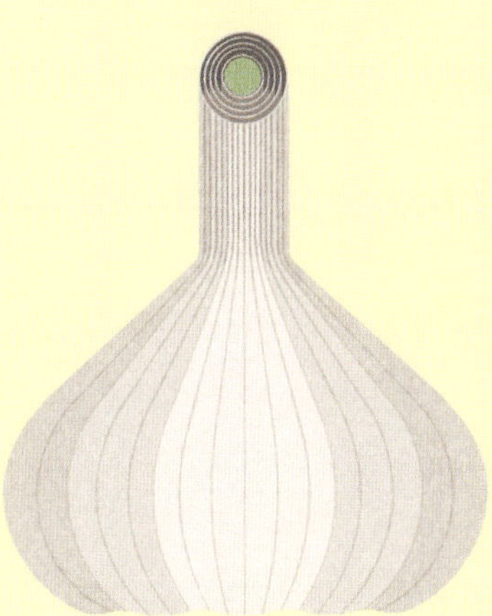

A World of Flavors

From medieval times well into the twentieth century, condiments were said to inflame lust and incite dangerous passions.

Condiments elevate food from the simple to the sublime, transforming bland dishes into objects of desire. Travelers are known to pack their own mini bottles of a favorite hot sauce, while immigrants and expats alike seek out the bottled flavors that remind them of home.

It's easy to forget that many of today's most familiar condiments were once considered exotic. During the Age of Exploration, European travelers developed a taste for piquant relishes like ketchups and chutneys. Once these seasonings were brought back home, they changed the Western diet in irrevocable ways by introducing a new range of flavors to complement familiar foods. These were the origins of such perennial favorites as Worcestershire sauce, bottled brown sauce, and steak sauce.

Because the mouth-filling flavors of condiments are often intensified by preserving, it seems only fitting to launch our series of small books on food preservation with a deep dive into condiments. In fact, the Latin root of the word, condire, means "to preserve or to season." *Condiment* originally referred to any substance that could keep food from spoiling; thus, salt is the original condiment. Over time the term came to refer to various preparations that yield concentrated flavors from salting, fermenting, pickling, and drying. Condiments have a long shelf life both by definition and by design. They are also generally healthful additions to the meal. Apart from various fish sauces, most are plant-based, and their preservative action, when it results from fermentation, adds beneficial microbes to the gut microbiome. By making condiments, the human hand forestalls decay on multiple levels.

Partly because they give rise to pleasure, spicy condiments imported from afar soon became objects of resistance and controversy. From medieval times well into the twentieth century, religious and secular moralists in both Europe and America railed against the sensory stimulation that condiments provide, claiming that they inflame lust and incite dangerous passions. For ascetics, condiments are seen as excessive ornamentation, an unnecessary garnish to simple, God-given foods. James Joyce played on the association of pungent foods with temptation and the devil in his novel *Ulysses*: "God made food, the devil the cooks." And indeed, we still refer to highly seasoned foods as "deviled," thanks to their copious amounts of mustard and pepper, two of the world's oldest condiments.

Yet condiments were far too delicious to be suppressed. Then and now they offer a way to escape the monotony of subsistence diets. The anthropologist Sidney Mintz posited a "core-fringe" theory in which meals in agrarian societies generally consisted of a bland, starchy core complemented by a more palatable "fringe"—a condiment—to add piquancy, pungency, and zest. All true, but the concept of "fringe" discounts the essential role of condiments. Although core foods ensure sustenance, it is the "fringe" that makes the meal more than just bodily fuel. The often-vibrant colors of condiments offset the monochrome palettes of starches, and when sauces are chunky, they can add appealing texture to otherwise soft foods.

Equally important, condiments provide touchstones of cultural identity as people and their foodways migrate around the world. On page 74, chef Edward Lee recalls how his grandmother regaled unannounced guests with the preserved and pickled vegetables that she always kept in the refrigerator to enhance a bowl of quickly prepared rice; Vikram Doctor remembers his grandmother's vivid-orange mussel pickle and relates how after her death, his mother repurposed the small amount that remained. Both stories highlight the nurturing aspect of homemade condiments, where the sight and smell of a jar of pickles can trigger deep memory and encapsulate one's past. Condiments help to convey in a concentrated bite the essence of family histories, as well as the stories of how they traversed the globe.

Some of the recipes in this book are quick to make, while others take weeks or months of aging or fermentation to achieve peak flavor. But the beauty of condiments is that once they are made, they become your secret arsenal of flavor—your muse, so to speak—a global larder that will turn the most mundane dishes into an exhilarating meal. Preservation isn't merely an end in itself. It is also a beginning, a way to widen, deepen, and ramp up our cooking with prepared ingredients always on hand. Condiments allow us to mix and match different culinary cultures, adding a spoonful of harissa to Provençal aioli, or a dollop of Georgian adjika to a Chinese stir-fry. Like us, you may become someone who spoons some of these condiments straight from the jar into your mouth—they're that delicious. Though we offer serving suggestions for every recipe, we encourage you to experiment, to play with the wonderfully wide range of flavors presented here, and to devise your own electrifying combinations.

TAYLOR MALI

My Deepest Condiments

I send you my deepest condiments
was in no way what my old friend
meant to say or write or send
the night she penned a note to me
one week after my father died.
Not *condolences*, or *sentiments*,
she sent me her deepest condiments
instead, as if the dead have need
of relish, mustard, and ketchup
on the other side.

O, the word made me laugh
so hard out loud it hurt!
So wonderfully absurd,
and such a sweet relief
at a time when it seemed

only grief was allowed in
after my father's death,
sweet and simple laughter,
which is nothing more than
breath from so far deep inside

it often brings up with it tears.
And so I laughed and laughed
until my sides were sore.
And later still, I even cried
a little more.

MAKES 1 PINT *or* 475 MILLILITERS

Zhug

For its popular appeal, the spicy Yemeni cilantro sauce known as zhug has been described as "the next Sriracha." This condiment is indeed fiery hot with chile peppers, but it is also aromatic with spices and herbaceous notes of cilantro and parsley.

In Yemen, this condiment is known by its Arabic name, sahawiq, *which refers to the traditional method of preparation by pounding the herbs into a paste between two stones. Today, it is better known around the world by its Hebrew name of zhug. Between 1949 and 1950, thousands of Yemeni Jews were airlifted to Israel, where they introduced this treasured condiment to their new home. Zhug soon became a staple of Israeli cuisine, and over the past decade, thanks to the trendiness of Israeli food, zhug has become a fixture in Mediterranean and Middle Eastern restaurants.*

Zhug is usually served freshly made, when it tastes bold and vivacious. We take it a step further, fermenting the herbs and spices to transform the sauce slightly but meaningfully. Fermentation adds not only complexity but also a more entrenched heat as the sauce deepens from bright green to olive.

10 large garlic cloves, crushed
4 packed cups/120 g cilantro leaves (about 2 large bunches)
2 packed cups/120 g parsley leaves (about 1 large bunch)
12 serrano or green jalapeño chiles, stemmed and thinly sliced
2 teaspoons kosher salt
1 teaspoon ground cumin
1 teaspoon freshly ground black pepper
1 teaspoon ground coriander
½ teaspoon sumac powder
½ teaspoon Aleppo or other dried red pepper flakes
¼ teaspoon ground cardamom
2 tablespoons/30 ml freshly squeezed lime juice

In a food processor, pulse the garlic until finely minced. Add the cilantro, parsley, chiles, salt, cumin, black pepper, coriander, sumac, red pepper, cardamom, and lime juice.

Pulse to make a fine paste. Pack into a 1-pint/475 ml canning jar. There should be a bit of headspace between the mixture and the lid; if not, transfer the paste to a slightly larger container.

Place a piece of plastic wrap or parchment paper directly against the surface of the paste and screw the lid onto the jar loosely. Leave the zhug to ferment at room temperature, out of direct sunlight, for 7 to 10 days. To release any gas pressure that builds up, unscrew the lid a couple times a day for the first few days, replacing the lid each time. By day 7, the paste will have turned from a verdant green to a duskier hue. At this point, taste the zhug to determine whether you like its degree of acidity. If not, let it ferment a bit longer; it can take up to 2 weeks to fully develop in flavor.

When the zhug is ready, place a fresh piece of plastic wrap or parchment directly on the surface and close the lid tightly. It will keep for 6 months in the refrigerator.

SERVING SUGGESTIONS USE TO MARINATE FISH / MIX WITH CHICKPEAS OR OTHER LEGUMES FOR A HEARTY SALAD BASE / WHISK INTO OLIVE OIL OR GREEK YOGURT FOR A READY DIP

MAKES 3 PINTS *or* 1.4 LITERS

Piccalilli

This condiment has a more aristocratic history than its whimsical name might suggest. The earliest recipe for piccalilli can be found in a 1694 cookery manuscript by Lady Anne Blencowe, who attributes the recipe to a certain Lord Kilmory, who enjoyed some connection to the East India Company, which had arrived in India in 1608. Lady Anne charmingly titles the recipe "To Pickle Lila, an Indian Pickle."

But piccalilli is, more properly, an Anglo-Indian condiment, a glorious way to enliven English garden produce with aromatic spices from the Indian subcontinent. Lady Anne's recipe calls for cabbage, cauliflower, celery, radishes, green beans, and asparagus, along with copious amounts of garlic and ginger for heat. She additionally recommends using melons, cucumbers, and plums. No doubt Lady Anne enjoyed the services of cooks and scullery maids. She prescribes a laborious process of individually salting and drying each vegetable over the course of nine days before pickling.

Here we streamline the operation into a mere two days by soaking the vegetables overnight in a salt brine, then stirring them into a seasoned sauce. Turmeric and mustard turn the piccalilli vivid yellow, giving it a visual appeal as bright as its taste.

SPICED VINEGAR

¾ cup/175 ml dark malt vinegar
¾ cup/175 ml white wine vinegar
¼ cup/50 g sugar
1½ teaspoons allspice berries
1½ teaspoons whole black peppercorns
1 teaspoon fennel seed
½ teaspoon dried red pepper flakes
1 bay leaf

VEGETABLES AND PICKLING LIQUID

1 cup plus 2 tablespoons/162 g kosher salt, plus more as needed
10 ounces/300 g cauliflower, cut into small florets, coarse stalks removed
8 ounces/225 g peeled white pearl onions, quartered
4 ounces/125 g fresh fennel, cut into ½-inch/1.25 cm pieces
4 ounces/125 g green beans, trimmed and cut into ¼-inch/6 mm slices

MUSTARD SAUCE

4 tablespoons/60 g unsalted butter
4½ teaspoons mustard oil
2 teaspoons ground turmeric
1½ teaspoons caraway seed
1 teaspoon ground coriander
½ teaspoon yellow mustard seed
3 garlic cloves, microplaned
4½ tablespoons/35 g all-purpose flour
1¼ teaspoons mustard powder
1 apple, peeled, cored, and grated
Scant ½ cup/50 g gherkins or cornichons, cut into ¼-inch/6 mm slices
2 teaspoons capers, drained, rinsed, and coarsely chopped
4 green onions, green and white parts, very thinly sliced
Freshly ground black pepper
Salt

PREPARE THE SPICED VINEGAR: In a large saucepan, combine the dark malt vinegar, white wine vinegar, sugar, allspice berries, peppercorns, fennel seed, red pepper flakes, and bay leaf. Bring to a boil over medium heat, stirring until the sugar dissolves. Decrease the heat to a rapid simmer and cook, covered, for 10 minutes. Allow the vinegar to cool to room temperature, then refrigerate overnight. CONTINUED ▸

PICCALILLI CONTINUED

PREPARE THE VEGETABLES AND BRINE: Pour 2 quarts/2 liters of cold water into a large bowl. Add the salt and stir until it dissolves. Stir in the cauliflower, pearl onions, fennel, and green beans, mixing well. Place a piece of plastic wrap directly against the vegetables. Set a pie plate or other weight on top of the vegetables to make sure they remain submerged in the brine. Cover the bowl with another piece of plastic wrap and refrigerate for 24 hours.

The next day, remove the vegetables from the refrigerator. Drain and discard the salt brine. Place the vegetables in a large pot and cover them with cold water. Bring to a boil. Reduce the heat to low and simmer for 5 minutes; the vegetables should be cooked through but still be a bit crisp. Quickly drain and run cold water over them to stop the cooking. Once the vegetables are cool and well drained, transfer them to a large bowl.

MAKE THE MUSTARD SAUCE: Warm a medium saucepan over low heat. Add the butter and mustard oil to the pan and allow the butter to melt gently, then stir in the turmeric, caraway, coriander, and mustard seed and cook until fragrant, stirring constantly, about 30 seconds. Decrease the heat to very low and add the garlic, flour, and mustard powder. Cook for 5 minutes, stirring constantly so that the flour doesn't burn.

Strain the spices from the vinegar and whisk the vinegar into the butter mixture. Add the grated apple, gherkins, and capers and cook for 3 to 5 minutes, until the apple is well incorporated. Stir in the green onions and black pepper, then remove the pan from the heat. You should have a thick, brightly colored sauce. Pour the sauce over the drained vegetables and stir well, making sure all the vegetables are coated. Taste for seasoning, adding more black pepper or salt as needed.

Transfer the piccalilli into three sterilized 1-pint/475 ml jars. Either store in the refrigerator for up to 3 months or, for longer storage, process in a water bath using our Notes on Canning (page 99). Wait at least one week before using to allow the flavors to intensify.

SERVING SUGGESTIONS SERVE AS A RELISH ON A DELI MEAT PLATTER OR WITH COOKED MEATS / SLATHER ON A SANDWICH / PURÉE INTO A MARINADE FOR CHICKEN OR VEGETABLES

MAKES 6 CUPS *or* 1.4 LITERS

Red Plum Hoisin Sauce

The precise origins of this thick, mahogany-colored sauce from Guangdong province in southern China have been lost to time. We do know that hoisin originally included dried or fermented seafood in addition to the wheat or black bean base, but as the sauce evolved, the seafood disappeared, no doubt because of its expense. What remains from the earliest forms is the essential thing, the sauce's wonderfully rich umami flavor coupled with a bit of sweet, spice, salt, and tang. To add a fruity note, our version uses dried red Angelino plums in addition to black bean sauce. These plums are widely available online or at specialty shops.

If you've already made the Black Bean Sauce on page 22, homemade hoisin sauce doesn't take long to prepare. But beware: once you taste it, you'll find it hard to use bottled sauce ever again.

2¼ cups/275 g dried red Angelino plums
1½ cups/360 ml vegetable stock
3 cups/600 g black bean sauce, homemade (page 22) or store bought
1¼ cups/300 ml sorghum syrup
1 cup/240 ml soy sauce
½ cup/120 ml unseasoned rice vinegar
¼ cup/25 g black garlic cloves, homemade (page 55) or store bought, peeled

Combine the dried plums in a small saucepan with enough vegetable stock to cover. Bring the mixture to a boil, then reduce the heat and simmer, uncovered, until the plums are plump and tender, 25 to 30 minutes. Drain the plums, reserving the liquid. Transfer the plums to a blender and purée until smooth.

In a large bowl, stir together the black bean sauce, sorghum syrup, soy sauce, rice vinegar, and black garlic cloves. Working in batches, add this mixture to the plum purée and blend until smooth. The sauce should be thick but spoonable. If desired, add some of the reserved liquid to thin it slightly.

Transfer the sauce to jars. It is ready to use as soon as it has cooled. Store in the refrigerator, where it will keep indefinitely.

SERVING SUGGESTIONS SERVE ALONGSIDE GRILLED MEATS / STIR INTO BUTTER SAUCES FOR A BRIGHT FINISH / USE AS A GLAZE FOR ROASTED CAULIFLOWER, BRUSSELS SPROUTS, OR WINTER SQUASH / MARINATE FISH IN THE SAUCE FOR 20 MINUTES BEFORE ROASTING, BROILING, OR GRILLING / ADD TO VEGETABLE STIR-FRIES

Harissa

The world enjoys so many thrilling hot sauces that we were initially hard put to decide which to include in this book. But harissa quickly jumped to the top of our list. Thanks to its copious herbs and warm spices, this North African hot-pepper paste yields more than heat, which comes on slowly only after the savor of spice. Here, we ferment the sweet and hot peppers for a week before concentrating them into a paste to make the flavor even more complex.

Although harissa is found throughout the Mahgreb of northwestern Africa, it probably originated in Tunisia. The peppers, of course, are native to the New World. After being introduced to Spain during the Columbian exchange, they were likely brought to North Africa by the Moriscos following their expulsion from Spain in the early seventeenth century. The word harissa *stems from the Arabic root* harīsa, *which means "to pound." Before the advent of food processors, the spices and peppers were laboriously pounded with a mortar and pestle, which some traditional cooks still use today.*

CHILE PASTE

2½ pounds/1.1 kg sweet red bell peppers, stemmed, seeded, and cut into large chunks
1 pound/454 g hot red chiles, such as cayenne, red jalapeño, or Fresno, stemmed
3 tablespoons/27 g kosher salt

HARISSA

1½ teaspoons coriander seed
1 teaspoon caraway seed
1 teaspoon fennel seed
1 teaspoon whole black peppercorns
½ teaspoon cumin seed
2½ tablespoons/17 g ground cayenne pepper or hot paprika, or more to taste
1 tablespoon sweet paprika
1 cup/240 ml extra-virgin olive oil
1 lightly packed cup/40 g fresh parsley leaves
½ lightly packed cup/8 g fresh dill
½ lightly packed cup/14 g fresh marjoram leaves, stripped from the stems
¾ lightly packed cup/9 g fresh mint leaves, stripped from the stems
¼ cup/43 g shallots, coarsely chopped
14 garlic cloves, coarsely chopped
2 tablespoons/30 g chopped preserved lemon, seeds removed
4 teaspoons freshly squeezed lemon juice
2½ tablespoons/38 ml sherry vinegar
2 teaspoons tomato paste
2 teaspoons honey
2 teaspoons kosher salt
1½ teaspoons sumac powder
1 teaspoon urfa biber (or substitute Aleppo pepper or chipotle chile powder)

MAKE THE CHILE PASTE: In a food processor, combine the bell peppers, red chiles, and salt and purée. Transfer the mixture to a 1-quart/1 L glass jar. Wipe the inside of the jar as clean as possible and press a piece of plastic wrap directly against the surface of the peppers to prevent mold growth. Cover the jar with a tight-fitting lid.

Leave the peppers to ferment on the countertop at 65° to 70°F/18° to 21°C for 1 week, checking back every couple of days and gently pressing a spoon against the plastic wrap to release any trapped CO_2 from the jar. If any white mold appears on the surface, simply scrape it off. After 1 week, the peppers should taste gently sour. If they aren't sufficiently sour, continue to ferment the peppers, checking on them daily.

Pour the peppers into a 9 by 13-inch/24 by 36 cm baking dish and smooth the surface (the mixture should be no more than 1 inch/ 2.5 cm deep). Transfer to a dehydrator set at 110°F/43°C, stirring every 4 to 6 hours, or cover and bake at 170°F/77°C, stirring occasionally after the mixture has begun to thicken. The peppers are ready when they have turned into a thick, concentrated paste, 12 to 16 hours in a dehydrator or 10 to 12 hours in an oven; you should have approximately 1½ cups/ 350 ml. At this point, if you aren't ready to finish, transfer the paste to a nonreactive container and refrigerate for up to 1 week.

FINISH THE HARISSA: In a spice grinder, combine the coriander, caraway, fennel, peppercorns, and cumin. Grind to a fine powder and combine with the ground cayenne and sweet paprika.

Gently warm the oil in a medium saucepan over low heat. Add the spices and cook, swirling occasionally, until very fragrant, 5 minutes. Cool to room temperature.

In a blender, purée the cooled oil with the parsley, dill, marjoram, mint, shallots, garlic, preserved lemon, and lemon juice. Return this mixture to the saucepan, set over medium-low heat, and whisk in the chile paste, sherry vinegar, tomato paste, honey, salt, sumac, and urfa biber. Cook, stirring frequently to prevent scorching, until the mixture is very thick and most of the liquid has cooked out, about 10 to 15 minutes. Purée in the blender once more until the harissa is perfectly smooth and emulsified. Use immediately or refrigerate in an airtight container for up to 1 year.

SERVING SUGGESTIONS RUB ONTO CHICKEN JUST BEFORE ROASTING / MIX WITH AN EQUAL AMOUNT OF AIOLI FOR AN UNCTUOUS DIPPING SAUCE / STIR INTO BEAN STEWS OR BEEF BROTH FOR A FIERY KICK / TURN INTO A COMPOUND BUTTER FOR STEAKS OR ROAST VEGETABLES / MIX WITH A LITTLE OIL AND STIR INTO COUSCOUS OR RICE BEFORE SERVING

MAKES ABOUT 1 PINT *or* 475 MILLILITERS

Adjika

This lively, salsa-like condiment has it all: heat, spice, and the zing of fresh herbs. Adjika originated in the western regions of Georgia—the country in the Caucasus, not the American state—where it was traditionally, and laboriously, made in a mortar and pestle. But today a food processor makes quick work of the task. Adjika remains such an iconic Georgian seasoning that UNESCO *has designated it as part of the country's "intangible cultural heritage."*

8 large garlic cloves, peeled and left whole
4 ounces/115 g fresh hot red chiles, such as cayenne or bird's eye, stemmed and seeded
1 large red bell pepper, stemmed and seeded
1 large celery rib, including leaves
2 cups/30 g coarsely chopped fresh dill
1½ cups/34 g coarsely chopped cilantro
⅓ cup/10 g coarsely chopped basil
¾ teaspoon ground coriander seed
½ teaspoon ground fenugreek (preferably blue)
½ teaspoon ground summer savory
¼ cup/60 ml red wine vinegar
¾ teaspoon kosher salt

Pulse the garlic in a food processor until finely chopped. Coarsely chop the chiles, bell pepper, and celery and add to the garlic. Pulse again. Add the dill, cilantro, basil, coriander seed, fenugreek, and summer savory and pulse to a medium-fine consistency.

Transfer the mixture along with any liquid to a bowl and stir in the vinegar and salt. Cover and let stand at room temperature overnight before packing into jars. Store in the refrigerator for up to 6 months. For longer storage, transfer to canning jars and process in a boiling water bath (see Notes on Canning, page 99).

SERVING SUGGESTIONS SERVE WITH GRITS / USE ALONGSIDE GRILLED MEATS OR AS A TOPPING FOR BURGERS / STIR INTO SOUPS FOR A FINISHING TOUCH / MIX WITH SOUR CREAM TO MAKE A DIP FOR CHIPS OR CRUDITÉS

MAKES 6 CUPS *or* 1.2 KILOGRAMS

Black Bean Sauce

If you love intense flavors, this sauce is for you. At its base are the dried, fermented black soybeans known as douchi, *which are made by inoculating the beans with koji mold and then leaving them to ferment with fresh ginger for six months or so. Douchi is an ancient food dating back to the Han dynasty, about 2,500 years ago. An archaeological dig of a noblewoman's tomb in China's Hunan province revealed a sealed jar of the beans that was carbon dated to 165 BCE. Luckily, you don't have to excavate your own douchi; you can easily find it in Asian markets and online. For an even more pronounced flavor, use dashi instead of vegetable stock.*

1 pound/454 g fermented black soybeans (douchi)
½ cup/120 ml grapeseed oil
7 tablespoons/105 ml sesame oil, half toasted and half untoasted
1½ heads (about 4 ounces/110 g) garlic, minced
About 5 ounces/140 g fresh ginger, peeled and minced
12 large green onions, white and green parts, thinly sliced
2 cups/475 ml vegetable stock or dashi
3 tablespoons/45 ml mirin
3 tablespoons/45 ml soy sauce
2 tablespoons/30 ml Shaoxing rice wine or fine dry sherry
2 tablespoons/30 ml unseasoned rice vinegar
⅔ cup/75 g sambal
2 firmly packed tablespoons/24 g light brown sugar

In a food processor, briefly whir the black beans until they are slightly broken. Be careful not to turn them into a purée—you want to leave some texture. Set aside.

In a 12-inch/30 cm skillet, combine the grapeseed and sesame oils over medium heat until they shimmer. Add the garlic and ginger and sauté for 1 to 2 minutes, until the garlic is translucent but not browned. Stir in the green onions and cook for 1 minute more. Add the vegetable stock, mirin, soy sauce, rice wine, rice vinegar, sambal, brown sugar, and black beans. Simmer the mixture, uncovered, over medium heat for 12 to 15 minutes, until it has thickened (there will still be some oil on the surface). Don't let all the liquid evaporate; the beans will thicken as they cool.

Cool the sauce to room temperature before transferring to a jar. It keeps well in the refrigerator for 6 months.

SERVING SUGGESTIONS TOSS WITH STIR-FRIED NOODLES OR VEGETABLES / MAKE A SAUCE FOR SAUTÉED WILD MUSHROOMS / WARM AND SERVE ALONGSIDE WHOLE COOKED FISH

MUSTARD

Mustard is a class-conscious condiment. French kings retained personal mustard makers to prepare the brown paste to their satisfaction, while yellow ballpark mustard remains the American everyman's dream. Depending on your taste, you can spoon mustard from a finely crafted porcelain pot or squeeze it from a bright plastic bottle. In its various forms, mustard has been appreciated since ancient times, enjoyed by Egyptians, Greeks, and Romans alike. In *De Re Rustica*, the first-century agronomist Columella describes a fine white mustard made by grinding the seeds, rinsing them with saltpeter, then activating them with white vinegar before adding finely ground pine nuts and almonds for thickening. Other Roman recipes describe sweet mustards seasoned with honey and olive oil.

The Romans introduced mustard seed to northern Europe when Julius Caesar conquered Gaul. Centuries passed before its cultivation took hold, but by the fourteenth century the production of prepared mustard was widespread. The once-venerable French Grey Poupon traces its lineage back to France in 1777. When the brand launched in the US in 1981, a television commercial featured an upper-crust man enjoying the Dijon mustard in his Rolls-Royce. But times change. Grey Poupon is not even French any longer, but owned by the huge conglomerate Kraft Heinz and manufactured in Michigan.

Cultural considerations aside, the differences among various mustards are profound, depending on the seeds that are used. All members of the cabbage family, mustard seeds can be yellow (also known as white), brown, or black. The liquid that the seeds are mixed with to form the paste varies, too, though it is generally something acidic, like vinegar, verjuice, or wine. The paste can be made mild or hot, depending on whether the seeds are processed when dry or wet, or with hot liquids or cold.

Grey Poupon, for instance, is made with brown mustard seeds ground fine and mixed with white wine to yield a creamy, light brown condiment, while ballpark mustard is made from yellow seeds mixed with vinegar and turmeric to achieve a vivid color. The inherent potency of the mustard seed is clear from its etymology: The word comes from the Latin *mustum arden*, or "burning must" (must being freshly pressed grapes). If a Frenchman gets angry—what we might call hot under the collar—he is likely to say "la moutarde me monte au nez" ("mustard is going up my nose").

Nonculinary uses for mustard's powerful heat range from the beneficial to the horrific, from mustard plasters applied to relieve congestion to mustard gas, deployed widely and lethally in World War I. Some high-performance athletes believe that mustard relieves muscle cramps; its effectiveness in easing joint pain is well established. Back in the kitchen, mustard's antimicrobial properties mean that it has useful applications as a preservative, one reason that the seeds are often added to chutneys and relishes around the world.

Mustard production was for centuries a laborious process, but in 1814 the Englishman Jeremiah Colman invented a method to manufacture a fine, dry, powdered mustard. Previously, mustard seeds had been crushed with a mortar and pestle, resulting in a coarse, grainy powder that was often mixed into balls along with spices like cinnamon and cloves and a binding agent such as vinegar, honey, or mashed raisins. In the seventeenth century, a type of mustard ball containing horseradish was devised in the town of Tewkesbury, England. So pungent was this mustard that "Tewkesbury mustard pills" became the slang term for fireballs, incendiary devices used to start fires.

The year 2022 may go down as the year of the great mustard catastrophe, when global supply chains dried up due to pandemic disruptions, the war in Ukraine, and climate change. In France, mustard virtually disappeared from the store shelves, provoking a national crisis. Until then, mustard had been taken for granted. French consumers didn't realize that these days most of the mustard seed used in such famous brands as Maille and Pommery are grown in western Canada, where a drought severely reduced the harvest, with global repercussions felt not only in France.

In many parts of the world, mustard is more esteemed than ketchup. For true mustard lovers, ketchup just doesn't "cut the mustard" as a condiment—it fails to provide that beloved fiery kick.

Photo (opposite): Mustard pot dating to 1770 from South Staffordshire, made from copper with enamel. The Metropolitan Museum of Art, New York, NY.

Photo (page 28): Mustard pot dating to 1760s from South Staffordshire, made from copper with enamel. The Metropolitan Museum of Art, New York, NY.

Photo (page 29): Mustard pot dating to 1740s from Meissen, made from hard paste porcelain. The Metropolitan Museum of Art, New York, NY.

MAKES ABOUT 1 PINT *or* 475 MILLILITERS

Honey Mustard

Mustard seeds are inherently sharp, so adding a sweetener like honey to basic mustard paste offsets the seeds' heat without masking their bite. We ferment our honey first to add another layer of complexity to this creamy, pale brown mustard. If you can find fresh mustard flowers, which bloom in early spring, they add an intriguing floral note, while dill or tarragon lends an appealing hint of herbs.

FERMENTED HONEY

⅔ cup/224 g raw honey
½ cup/120 ml mustard flowers (or dill or tarragon leaves stripped from the stems)
1 tablespoon water

MUSTARD

¼ cup/45 g whole yellow mustard seed
1½ tablespoons whole brown mustard seed
2 teaspoons whole black peppercorns
7 tablespoons/115 ml apple cider vinegar
¼ cup/110 g fermented honey (see above)
1 garlic clove, coarsely chopped
1 shallot, thinly sliced
2 teaspoons kosher salt

FERMENT THE HONEY: In a small jar, stir together the honey, mustard flowers, and water. Cover the jar with cheesecloth and place it in a clean, low-light area at a temperature of 60° to 68°F/16° to 20°C for 2 weeks, or until the honey is visibly thinner and a little bubbly. The flavor will be subtle. Strain the flowers or herbs from the honey. If not using right away, cap the jar tightly and refrigerate for up to 1 year.

MAKE THE MUSTARD: Combine the yellow and brown mustard seeds and peppercorns in an 8-ounce/240 ml jar and cover them with water. Seal with a lid and refrigerate for 24 hours. Once the seeds have plumped, drain the mustard seeds and peppercorns; discard the water.

Combine the vinegar, fermented honey, garlic, shallot, and salt in a blender. Pulse briefly to break up the solids, then blend on high until the mixture is smooth. Scrape down the sides of the blender and add the drained mustard seeds and peppercorns. Blend on low for 20 seconds, then increase the speed and blend until the mixture resembles mayonnaise. If you want a textured mustard, pulse the mixture just a bit longer; if you want the mustard to be smooth, continue to process until you reach the desired consistency.

Transfer the mustard to a 1-pint/475 ml jar and refrigerate it for 2 days before using. The mustard will keep in the refrigerator for 6 months.

SERVING SUGGESTIONS LAYER INTO A GRILLED HAM, CHEESE, AND APPLE SANDWICH / SERVE AS A DIPPING SAUCE FOR HOMEMADE SOFT PRETZELS / RUB ONTO A PORK ROAST 24 HOURS BEFORE COOKING

MAKES ABOUT ¾ CUP *or* 175 MILLILITERS

Gardal

This fiery hot mustard is a specialty of the Don Cossacks, a fiercely independent people known for their horsemanship and military prowess. Made from the pungent brown seeds of Brassica juncea, *gardal is an ideal accompaniment to the cured pork belly known as* salo. *The use of pickle brine distinguishes this mustard from others, which call for vinegar as the acidic element. Though the mustard takes just a few minutes to make, its flavor needs 24 hours to fully bloom.*

Gardal stores well in the refrigerator, though its heat tends to diminish over time. When it's newly made, however, be forewarned that a little goes a long way.

½ cup/90 g brown mustard seed
Generous ¼ teaspoon kosher salt
5 tablespoons/75 ml pickle brine (from lacto-fermented pickles, not vinegar-based ones)

In a spice grinder or mini food processor, grind the mustard seed to a fine powder. Transfer the powder to a bowl and stir in the salt. Add the pickle brine and mix well. Cover the bowl and leave the mustard to sit for 24 hours at warm room temperature for the flavor to develop. Transfer to a small jar and store in the refrigerator, where the mustard will keep indefinitely.

SERVING SUGGESTIONS SERVE THE CLASSIC WAY WITH SAUSAGES AND HOT DOGS / HEAT GENTLY WITH SOUR CREAM AND HERBS TO MAKE A SAUCE FOR GRILLED MEATS / MIX INTO EGG SALAD FOR ADDED PUNCH / RAMP UP VINAIGRETTES BY ADDING A SPOONFUL TO THE BASE

MAKES ABOUT 1 QUART *or* 1 LITER

Rémoulade

In its purest form, the classic French rémoulade is nothing more than mayonnaise blended with mustard and herbs. But the sauce gained fame as the elegant Céleri Rémoulade when it was paired with raw, grated celeriac. As rémoulade traveled the world, it morphed according to local tastes, with tangy additions like capers and pickles. In New Orleans, Francophone settlers introduced Creole Rémoulade Sauce, a pumped-up version spicy with cayenne or hot pepper sauce, to serve with shrimp and seafood dishes. In the American South, rémoulade's cousins include Mississippi Comeback, with ketchup for a sweeter profile, and Alabama White, made creamy with vinegar and horseradish. In Denmark, where the sauce is slathered on smørrebrød, *fish cakes, and hot dogs, remoulade has become a national condiment.*

Our rémoulade makes celeriac the star. We mix the grated root with carrots, onions, green beans, parsley, and dill before adding spices and leaving the colorful blend to ferment for a week. This robust combination is ready to pair with mayonnaise at a moment's notice for what is arguably the best rémoulade sauce you've ever tasted.

2 packed cups / 170 g peeled and coarsely grated or finely julienned celeriac
1 packed cup / 85 g coarsely grated or finely julienned carrots
½ cup / 65 g green beans trimmed into ¼-inch / 6 mm rounds
½ cup / 60 g thinly sliced sweet onion
½ cup / 30 g firmly packed fresh parsley leaves, coarsely chopped
½ cup / 8 g coarsely chopped fresh dill
¾ teaspoon mustard powder
¼ teaspoon toasted and ground caraway seed
¼ teaspoon toasted whole celery seed
1 tablespoon kosher salt

TO FINISH
Mayonnaise
Salt
Freshly ground black or white pepper

In a large bowl, combine all of the vegetables, herbs, mustard powder, caraway seed, celery seed, and kosher salt, and massage them well with your hands to incorporate the salt. Keep working the vegetables until they release moisture and become limp, about 5 minutes; liquid will begin to pool at the bottom of the bowl. Cover the mixture and set aside for 30 minutes.

Pack the vegetables and their liquid into a 1-quart / 1 L wide-mouth canning jar, pressing down firmly to remove any air pockets, until the mixture is completely submerged. Place a piece of parchment paper or plastic wrap directly on the vegetables and weight it with a plastic bag filled with water, a glass fermentation weight, or a clean rock to keep everything submerged. Cover the jar with a lid. Allow to ferment at room temperature (68° to 72°F / 20° to 22°C) for 1 to 2 weeks. Unscrew and gently re-screw the lid each day to release any gas.

Begin tasting the mixture after 7 days to see if it's sufficiently sour; the vegetables should be tangy but still have a bit of tooth to them. When they are ready, re-seal the jar with a tight-fitting lid and refrigerate until you plan to use the rémoulade.

TO MAKE THE RÉMOULADE: Remove a portion of the base from the jar and squeeze most of the brine from it. Mix with equal parts mayonnaise and season with salt and pepper to taste.

SERVING SUGGESTIONS SERVE ON FISH SANDWICHES OR WITH CRAB CAKES / USE AS A SAUCE FOR GRILLED ASPARAGUS / SERVE ALONGSIDE STEAMED ARTICHOKES

Herbes Salées

The Acadians, settlers of French origin in what is now the Maritime provinces and eastern Quebec, salt the fresh herbs of summer to summon brightness and supply vitamins during the long winter. The layers of salt provide texture, a bracing crunch followed by a hit of herbaceous salinity. According to the Slow Food Foundation for Biodiversity, the traditional ingredients for herbes salées *include leaves from various types of alliums, such as shallots and chives. Here we've expanded the herbal range to create an exceptionally aromatic seasoning that has the power to banish the chill of a frigid maritime breeze for a few fleeting moments. For a bright saline burst, blend this condiment into soups, chowders, or stews just before serving. Or rub it onto meat before grilling; some studies maintain that herbs minimize grilling's carcinogenic effects.*

1 cup/45 g chives, finely chopped
1 firmly packed cup/15 g fresh dill, finely chopped
1 firmly packed cup/60 g fresh parsley leaves, finely chopped
1 cup/40 g chervil, including tender stems, finely chopped
¼ cup/10 g tarragon leaves, finely chopped
1 cup/25 g other soft herbs, such as cilantro, mint, or celery leaves, finely chopped
1 cup/100 g finely chopped green onions
2 garlic cloves, finely minced
¾ cup/143 g medium-coarse salt, such as grey sea salt or fleur de sel

In a large bowl, combine the chives, dill, parsley, chervil, tarragon, other soft herbs, and green onions. Stir in the garlic. Layer 1 inch/2.5 cm of the herb mixture in the bottom of a 2-quart/2 L crock or glass bowl and sprinkle with some of the salt. Repeat the layers until all of the herb mixture and salt have been used. Cover and refrigerate for 2 to 3 weeks before using to meld the flavors. The herbs keep in the refrigerator for 6 months or more.

SERVING SUGGESTIONS GRIND INTO A PASTE TO SEASON MEATS BEFORE COOKING / STIR INTO SOUPS TO ADD AN HERBAL FINISH / USE TO SEASON A COMPOUND BUTTER FOR VEGETABLES OR MEATS

MAKES 1 PINT *or* 475 MILLILITERS

Beet Chrain

This ruby-red horseradish is well known to lovers of gefilte fish, who add a dollop to the mild fish quenelles to give them a kick and some dazzling color. Chrain is a Yiddish word that derives from khren, *Russian for "horseradish." Most American recipes for this beloved Eastern European condiment tame the fiery root, first by calling for twice as many beets as horseradish and then by boiling or roasting them to make the final product milder. Our recipe flips that script. We use twice as much horseradish as beets, and because we use a raw beet, it sharpens rather than softens the flavor. You may also swap yellow beets in for the red to make a golden version.*

Horseradish root varies in its degree of heat, depending on its age. So look for young roots that are firm and unbruised, neither desiccated nor too fibrous. In any case, take care not to breathe in too deeply when you open the lid of the food processor. Whether young or old, grated horseradish is potent enough to make your eyes sting.

8 ounces/225 g horseradish root, peeled and coarsely chopped
1 medium red beet (4 ounces/115 g), coarsely chopped
¼ cup/60 ml distilled white vinegar
1 tablespoon freshly squeezed lemon juice
1 tablespoon kosher salt
1 tablespoon sugar
¼ cup/60 ml warm water

In a food processor fitted with the shredding disk, shred the chopped horseradish and beet. Replace the disk with the chopping blade. Add the vinegar, lemon juice, salt, and sugar to the shredded roots and process the mixture until finely chopped. Add the water, continuing to process until the horseradish is very fine (the mixture will still have some texture). If the mixture seems too dry, add a little more water.

Pack the chrain into a 1-pint/475 ml jar and store in the refrigerator. Let it sit for at least 24 hours before using to allow the flavors to meld. The chrain will keep for 3 months, though its heat will diminish as it ages.

SERVING SUGGESTIONS SERVE WITH SMOKED WHITEFISH, EITHER STRAIGHT OR SOFTENED WITH SOUR CREAM / USE AS A TOPPING FOR SCHNITZEL OR OTHER BREADED CUTLETS

INDIAN PICKLES

When Madhur Jaffrey's grandmother made her famous lime pickle, a key step was hand-stirring the limes as the pickle matured. But not just any hand would do. "According to my grandmother, the chemistry of most hands would cause the pickle to rot," Jaffrey wrote in *Invitation to Indian Cooking*. Only Ishri, her grandfather's manservant, was judged to have the right hand to reach in, once a month, "to give the pickles a 'swish.'"

Indian condiments come with many such rituals and superstitions. The grinding stones and slabs used to pulverize spices for pickling to make spiced powders like podis (also called "gunpowder") or fresh spice pastes like chutneys play a role in traditional Indian wedding ceremonies. Doling out pickles from their tightly sealed jars was a job guarded by family matriarchs, who trusted no one else to dig in their spoons.

Condiments matter because, all too often, they are the main interest in a meal. The foreign image of an Indian meal made up of multiple stews, dhals, fried snacks, and grilled meat or fish, perhaps all combined in a lavish thali meal, is far from the reality of a country where daily hunger is still far too common.

For many people in India, a meal is still primarily carbohydrates, like heaps of rice or rotis made with wheat or millet. There might be dhal or sabzi (vegetables), but there will always be at least one condiment, even if just a raw red onion. Rotis and pickles are packed for rail journeys, easy to eat without a mess. Khichdi, the lentils and rice combination that is perhaps the most emblematic Indian meal, is said in a common rhyme to have char yaar (four friends): dahi (yogurt), papad (poppadums), ghee, achar (pickles).

Achar differs from pickles made in most other parts of the world, which use salt and acids, like vinegar, to prevent growth of bacteria and mold. Indian pickles are primarily made with oil which, at best, seeps up to the surface and serves as an air lock. This explains the care needed in spooning them out because it risks breaking the air lock. Superstitions remind people to be careful, or a whole batch can go bad.

There are benefits to pickling with oil. Oil helps mouthfeel, making pickles lushly textured. Some oils, like pungent mustard, add their own flavor. Above all, the flavor compounds in most spices are oil-soluble, so pickling in oil diffuses the flavor better. *Achar-ras*, the pickle "juice" or spiced oil, is used as a flavoring ingredient in recipes. It is drizzled on bread for the pickle sandwiches Indian parents insist will ruin their kids' digestion, but it tastes too good not to eat. Oil ekes out the flavor of the pickled ingredient even when that has been finished.

That's what my mother did with the last batch of her grandmother's famous mussel pickle. After my great-grandmother died, my mother strictly allowed herself—and certainly not us children—a daily dose of one deeply orange-tinged pickled mussel. Then she cut carrots and submerged them in the leftover oil, to simulate what she knew she would never taste again.

VIKRAM DOCTOR
Journalist and podcast host, Goa, India

Gooseberry Achar

The magisterial Usha's Pickle Digest *includes recipes for thirty-two different gooseberry pickles ranging from spicy to sweet. In India, the gooseberry, or amla, is prized in Ayurvedic medicine for its ability to keep the bodily humors in balance—its very name derives from the Sanskrit word for "nectar of life." Though we might think of nectars as ambrosial, the Indian gooseberry is in fact bitter and sour, making it a favorite choice for pickles and chutneys. For this pungent achar, we use either gooseberries or cape gooseberries, which we preserve not in salt (like the preserved lime achar on page 48) but in oil.*

3 tablespoons/45 ml grapeseed oil
1 tablespoon mustard oil
¼ teaspoon asafoetida (hing) powder
10 ounces/312 g fresh gooseberries, stemmed, or cape gooseberries, outer husks removed
¼ cup/60 ml regular, untoasted sesame oil
1 tablespoon toasted sesame oil
4 garlic cloves, finely minced
2 to 3 tablespoons/15 to 23 g red chile powder, preferably Kashmiri
2 tablespoons/22 g yellow or brown mustard seed, semi-finely ground
1 tablespoon kosher salt, plus more as needed
1 teaspoon turmeric powder
¼ teaspoon fenugreek seed, semi-finely ground
¼ teaspoon whole cumin seed
¼ teaspoon whole anise seed
1½ tablespoons freshly squeezed lemon juice

In a small saucepan over low heat, warm the grapeseed and mustard oils. Add the asafoetida and stir to combine. Remove the oil from the heat and set aside to cool completely at room temperature.

Rinse the gooseberries well and wipe them dry with a clean kitchen towel. Cut a slit in each one with the tip of a knife so that the berries do not burst while cooking.

In a medium saucepan over medium-low heat, warm the untoasted and toasted sesame oils until shimmering. Stir in the gooseberries, mixing well. Cover the pan and cook over low heat for about 2 minutes for gooseberries, or 8 to 10 minutes for cape gooseberries, stirring halfway through, until the gooseberries are soft but still retain their shape. Do not let them brown.

Turn off the heat and stir the garlic into the pan. Set aside for 10 minutes to allow the garlic to infuse into the oil. Rewarm the mixture over low heat and stir in the chile powder, mustard seed, salt, tumeric, fenugreek, cumin, and anise. Cook for 2 to 3 minutes over low heat, stirring occasionally, so that the spices bloom but don't burn.

Remove the pan from the heat and leave the gooseberries to cool to room temperature. Once the mixture has cooled, stir in the lemon juice. Taste for seasoning, adding more salt if desired.

Spoon the gooseberries into a 1-pint/475 ml jar, pressing down on them with the back of a spoon. Immediately pour the cooled asafoetida oil into the jar over the gooseberries. Some of the oil will make its way into the nooks and crannies of the pickle, while some will float on top. Make sure that the oil covers the pickle completely to seal it. Cover the jar with a lid and let the pickle mature for 3 to 4 days at room temperature before eating. Refrigerate the achar after opening. It will keep for 3 months.

SERVING SUGGESTIONS SERVE ALONGSIDE ALL MANNER OF CURRIES / MIX INTO YOGURT FOR A SPICY DIPPING SAUCE OR MARINADE / PURÉE UNTIL SMOOTH AND USE TO SEASON LAMB OR PORK MEATBALLS

MAKES 1 QUART *or* 1 LITER

Preserved Lime Achar

Achar *is a catchall term in South Asia for pickles that have been preserved in either oil or brine. After discovering them in India, British sailors carried these long-lasting preserves on their voyages to alleviate the monotony of salt beef and hardtack. Achar is enjoyed in Malaysia and parts of Africa, as well as in Japan, where summer vegetables soaked in a sweet-and-sour, chile-infused marinade are known as* achara-zuke. *Achar even made its way to the Lowcountry of the American South, where it was christened "Ats Jaar." Achar's widespread appeal is clear from the etymology listed in the venerable* Oxford English Dictionary: *"Probably of multiple origins. A borrowing from Persian. Probably partly also a borrowing from Portuguese. Probably partly also a borrowing from Dutch. Probably partly also a borrowing from Malay."*

The preserved limes are intensely aromatic—their fragrance alone induces salivation. Once the limes are steamed, we mix them with spices for an irresistible pickle.

6 cups/875 g Preserved Limes (recipe follows), drained and liquid reserved (or substitute store-bought preserved lemons)
½ teaspoon whole black peppercorns
1 teaspoon coriander seed
½ teaspoon caraway seed
½ teaspoon dill seed
½ teaspoon cumin seed
1 tablespoon kosher salt
½ teaspoon sweet paprika
½ teaspoon anise seed
½ teaspoon onion powder
¼ teaspoon ground turmeric
¼ teaspoon cayenne pepper
6 tablespoons/90 ml reserved brine from limes
¼ cup/85 g honey, preferably raw
¼ cup/60 ml grapeseed oil
1 onion, thinly sliced
2 garlic cloves, minced
½ serrano chile, including seeds, stemmed and finely minced or grated on a microplane

Pour 2 to 3 inches/5 to 8 cm of water into a steamer pan, place the steamer rack above the water, and set the drained limes on the rack. Cover, bring to a boil over medium heat, and steam until the limes can be pierced by a skewer, about 10 minutes. Remove the limes from the steamer. When cool enough to handle, cut them into ½-inch/1.25 cm pieces.

In a mortar or spice grinder, finely grind the peppercorns, coriander, caraway, dill, and cumin seeds. Transfer to a small bowl and stir in the salt, paprika, anise seed, onion powder, turmeric, and cayenne. Gradually add the reserved brine and the honey, stirring to dissolve.

Heat a 10-inch/25 cm skillet over medium heat until a drop of water flicked on the surface sizzles gently on contact. Add the oil and immediately stir in the onion, garlic, and serrano. Cook, stirring occasionally, until the vegetables are slightly softened but not browned, about 5 minutes. Add the spice mixture to the skillet and bring to a simmer while stirring. Add the chopped limes and cook, uncovered, over medium-low heat until reduced to a thick paste, about 5 minutes. Let cool.

Transfer to small jars and cap tightly. The achar can be used as soon as it has cooled. It will keep for up to 6 months in the refrigerator.

SERVING SUGGESTIONS FINELY CHOP AND MIX INTO GREEK YOGURT FOR A RAITA-STYLE SAUCE / SERVE ALONGSIDE FRIED FISH AND RICE / TOSS WITH SMASHED PAN-FRIED POTATOES

PRESERVED LIMES

1 cup/140 g kosher salt
1 teaspoon caraway seed, toasted and ground
1 teaspoon dill seed, toasted and ground
1 teaspoon coriander seed, toasted and ground
2 green serrano chiles, stemmed and minced
4 garlic cloves, minced
1 tablespoon fresh ginger, peeled and minced
1 tablespoon ground turmeric, or 3 tablespoons fresh turmeric juice
2 pounds/910 g limes
4 to 4½ cups/950 ml to 1 L freshly squeezed or bottled lime juice

In a small bowl, stir together the salt, caraway seed, dill seed, coriander seed, chiles, garlic, ginger, and ground turmeric (if using turmeric juice, reserve to add later).

Trim the stems from the limes, taking care not to cut into the flesh. Using a paring knife and starting at the stem end, cut each lime into four wedges, cutting down to, but not through, the base. Working with one lime at a time, hold it over a bowl, gently pry it open, and fill with the salt mixture, capturing in the bowl any of the mixture that fails to adhere. Pack the salted limes, along with any salt remaining in the bowl, into a sterilized 2-quart/2 L canning jar. If using turmeric juice, pour it into the jar. Pour in enough lime juice to cover the limes completely.

Seal the jar and place it in a clean, low-light area with an ambient temperature of 60° to 68°F (16° to 20°C). Leave the limes to sit for about 6 weeks, turning the jar upside down occasionally to prevent the growth of mold. The limes are ready when the peels look slightly translucent and are soft enough to pierce easily with a knife; they taste best when left to mature for 3 months before serving. Transfer the jar to the refrigerator, where the limes will keep for up to 1 year.

MAKES 1 PINT *or* 475 MILLILITERS

Ginger-Sesame Chutney

The word chutney *is the anglicized form of the Hindi* chatni, *which refers to a wide variety of relishes used to enhance meals throughout the Indian subcontinent. The British, who colonized India for nearly one hundred years, popularized chutney in the West in the nineteenth century. Chutneys are wonderfully versatile, since they can be made from all sorts of vegetables, herbs, and fruits mixed with spices. Their flavors are highly regional, ranging from hot and spicy to sour and sweet, depending on local tastes and ingredients. This ginger-sesame chutney is a specialty of the state of Andhra Pradesh in the northern part of South India. It tastes more sour than sweet, due to a generous amount of tamarind paste. And it's healthful besides. Traditional Ayurvedic practice considers ginger a universal medicine, thanks to its ability to aid digestion, stimulate circulation, reduce joint pain, and counter inflammation.*

5 tablespoons plus 2 teaspoons/85 ml regular, untoasted sesame oil
1 large sweet onion, thinly sliced
1¼ cups/120 g peeled and minced fresh ginger
3 large garlic cloves, minced
2 or 3 fresh green chile peppers, such as serrano, stemmed and chopped with seeds
1 or 2 dried red chile peppers, such as chile de árbol, stemmed and torn
1¼ teaspoons black mustard seed
1¼ teaspoons cumin seed
Zest of 1 large lime
Zest of 1 lemon
¼ cup/35 g white sesame seeds
5 tablespoons/50 g tamarind paste
2½ tablespoons/35 g grated jaggery or firmly packed light brown sugar
1½ teaspoons kosher salt

In a medium sauté pan, warm 5 tablespoons/75 ml of the sesame oil over medium-low heat until it begins to shimmer. Add the onion and cook until softened and blond, 8 to 10 minutes, stirring frequently. Stir in the ginger, increase the heat to medium-high, and cook the mixture, stirring, until golden, 5 to 8 minutes. Using a slotted spoon, transfer the onion and ginger to a blender, leaving the oil in the pan.

Return the pan to the burner and add the garlic and green and red chiles to the remaining oil. Cook over medium heat for 1 to 2 minutes, stirring frequently, until the garlic is golden. Scrape the mixture to one side and add the remaining 2 teaspoons of sesame oil to the pan. Drop the mustard and cumin seeds into the oil and immediately cover the pan. Reduce the heat to low and cook for about 30 seconds, just until the sputtering diminishes.

Stir in the citrus zests and sesame seeds and warm for a minute or two. Transfer to the blender along with the tamarind paste, jaggery, and salt. Purée and taste for seasoning.

Spoon the hot chutney into a sterilized 1-pint/475 ml canning jar, leaving ½-inch/1.25 cm of headspace. For long keeping, process the chutney in a boiling water bath using our Notes on Canning (page 99); otherwise leave it to cool at room temperature, then store in the refrigerator. Allow the flavors to meld for a few days before using. The chutney will keep, refrigerated, for at least 3 months.

SERVING SUGGESTIONS USE AS A DIPPING SAUCE FOR WHOLE GRILLED FISH, SUCH AS MACKEREL, SARDINES, OR BRANZINO / LAYER INTO GRILLED CHEESE SANDWICHES / BAKE WITH HALLOUMI CHEESE IN A CAST-IRON PAN UNTIL TENDER

MAKES ABOUT 1 PINT *or* 475 MILLILITERS

Black Garlic Barbecue Sauce

This dazzling barbecue sauce has taken a circuitous cultural path throughout the world. For centuries cooks in Korea, Japan, and Thailand have appreciated black garlic for both its culinary appeal and its healthful antioxidant properties. When fresh heads of garlic are heated, they soften and blacken as enzymes transform their sharp flavor, turning it sweet and giving it a deep umami punch. Here, we add black garlic to a vinegar-based barbecue sauce, whose own history traces back to West Africa, the Caribbean, and the American colonies. The indigenous Taíno of the Caribbean prepared the original barbecue by slowly smoking meat on racks over wood. After African slaves introduced a taste for acid and heat, lime juice and native peppers served as an early condiment to the smoked meat. Barbecue gradually spread to the southeastern seaboard of North America, where the colonists substituted vinegar for lime juice and added additional seasonings and sugar. The midnight-black sauce we offer here is tangy and savory, a perfect melding of flavors that reflect its peripatetic evolution. This sauce works equally well as a marinade or as a finishing sauce for meats and vegetables, no matter where you happen to be in the world.

If you want to make your own black garlic, look for plump heads of garlic with large cloves, and be sure to begin the process a good month before you plan to make the sauce.

8 ounces/ 225 g black garlic cloves, homemade (recipe follows) or store bought
1 ounce/28 g raw garlic, cloves peeled
1 cup/240 ml unseasoned rice vinegar
2½ tablespoons/35 ml balsamic vinegar
1½ tablespoons brown sugar
3¼ teaspoons/17 ml grapeseed oil
3¼ teaspoons/17 ml extra-virgin olive oil
2¼ teaspoons honey
2¼ teaspoons kosher salt
Freshly ground black pepper

In a blender, combine the black garlic, raw garlic, rice vinegar, balsamic vinegar, brown sugar, grapeseed oil, olive oil, honey, salt, and black pepper. Purée until smooth. If not using immediately, transfer to an airtight container and refrigerate for up to 3 months.

SERVING SUGGESTIONS SLATHER ON PORK OR BEEF RIBS, BEFORE AND AFTER COOKING / USE TO COAT GRILLED BRASSICAS / MIX WITH CHOPPED GREEN ONIONS AND A BIT OF SESAME OIL FOR A DIPPING SAUCE

HOMEMADE BLACK GARLIC

You can use a dehydrator, slow cooker, or rice cooker to make black garlic.

1 pound / 454 g whole heads garlic, unpeeled

Wrap the unpeeled garlic heads in plastic wrap to trap humidity and prevent the garlic from drying out. Then wrap them in several layers of aluminum foil. If using a dehydrator, hold the garlic at 130°F / 55°C until the heads are soft and have turned shiny black, about 3 weeks. If using a rice warmer or slow cooker, place a thick layer of aluminum foil on the bottom of the appliance to insulate the garlic from too much heat, then add the wrapped heads. Set the appliance on its "warm" setting (not the cook or "low" setting). The garlic can take up to 3 weeks to transition from white to black, but begin checking it after 10 days by unwrapping one head to examine the cloves, since you want to make sure they don't dry out—they should be nice and plump. If, after 3 weeks, the garlic is still not soft and black, keep heating it for another week or so, until blackened and tender.

Store the garlic in an airtight container at room temperature for up to 6 months. Peel the cloves before using.

Worcestershire Sauce

Like many condiments, Worcestershire sauce—a savory blend of anchovies, tamarind, malt vinegar, molasses, and spices—is the product of colonialism. Its roots lie in India, and if we're to believe the creation myth surrounding its discovery, the sauce was introduced by an English nobleman who returned from Bengal and implored the Worcester apothecarists John Lea and William Perrins to recreate his favorite sauce. Unhappy with the result, Lea and Perrins set the strong-smelling concoction aside and forgot about it until they were tidying up their cellar and found that the mixture had aged into a delectable sauce. Lea & Perrins began selling Worcestershire sauce in 1837, advertising their product as much for its digestive properties as for its taste. In 1839 the sauce became the first commercially bottled condiment imported into the United States, and it has been a staple ever since. By giving it an English place name and a legendary beginning, Lea and Perrins turned a sauce of dubious origin into a popular domestic product.

2 tablespoons/36 g chopped dried figs or raisins
1 cup/240 ml malt vinegar
¼ cup/60 ml soy sauce
¼ cup/80 g unsulfured molasses (not blackstrap)
2 tablespoons/20 g tamarind paste
1 ounce/30 g anchovies in oil, drained and chopped
1 small yellow onion, coarsely chopped
1½ teaspoons tomato paste
½-inch/1.25 cm piece fresh ginger, peeled and chopped
3 to 4 garlic cloves, crushed
4 teaspoons celery salt
1 firmly packed tablespoon dark brown sugar or maple syrup
1 chile de árbol, stemmed and chopped
Zest of ½ lemon
1½ teaspoons mustard powder
½ teaspoon curry powder
½ teaspoon whole cloves
½ teaspoon whole black peppercorns
½-inch/1.25 cm piece stick cinnamon, or ¼ teaspoon ground cinnamon
1 cardamom pod, cracked

In a small bowl, pour boiling water over the figs. Let sit for 15 minutes to soften, then drain.

Combine the figs, ½ cup/120 ml of the malt vinegar, the soy sauce, molasses, tamarind paste, anchovies, onion, tomato paste, ginger, and garlic in a food processor. Process until smooth.

Pour the puréed mixture into a medium saucepan and add the remaining ½ cup/120 ml malt vinegar, the celery salt, brown sugar, chile, lemon zest, mustard powder, curry powder, cloves, peppercorns, cinnamon, and cardamom pod. Bring to a boil, then remove from the heat.

Pour the mixture into a 1-pint/475 ml canning jar, filling it right to the top. Seal with a lid and store in a cool, dark place for at least 1 month before using (the longer it stands, the stronger the flavor will become).

Once the sauce has aged, strain it through a fine-mesh sieve into small jars, preferably of dark glass. (You can save the solids to flavor soups or stews or dry them into a salty powder.) Shake the jars gently before using. The sauce keeps indefinitely in the refrigerator.

SERVING SUGGESTIONS ADD TO CAESAR SALAD DRESSING OR COCKTAIL SAUCE / BRUSH ON STEAKS BEFORE GRILLING / PUT A FEW DASHES IN SOUP BASES FOR AN EXTRA LAYER OF FLAVOR / SHAKE A FEW DROPS INTO BLOODY MARYS

KETCHUP

The thick, sweet, red condiment that brightens French fries and hot dogs didn't always look or taste as it does today. Ketchup actually evolved from the fermented fish sauces of Southeast Asia, which British sailors encountered on their voyages to Sumatra and Java in the seventeenth century. There they tasted pungent *ke-tchup* or *kecap*, brown in color and having the consistency of soy sauce. By the early eighteenth century, Britons had embraced the condiment. It was especially popular with homemakers who made savory ketchups with ingredients like mushrooms, oysters, green walnuts, and grapes. In her 1747 cookbook, *The Art of Cookery Made Plain and Easy*, Hannah Glasse offers a recipe "To make catchup to keep twenty years." She calls for a gallon of strong stale beer, two quarts of mushrooms, a pound of shallots, mace, cloves, peppercorns, ginger, and a pound of anchovies.

Similar recipes eventually made their way into American cookbooks. In 1812 a Philadelphia scientist named James Mease published the first known recipe for tomato ketchup, using the native American ingredient he called "love apples." With neither spices nor vinegar, Mease's ketchup was more akin to tomato sauce, but it gained ground as a seasoning for soups and stews. Such early tomato ketchups were fermented; only later did commercial producers begin to load up on vinegar and sugar so that the condiment could be stored for long keeping without fear of a sour taste or exploding bottles—two problems that incorrectly fermented ketchup posed.

Although ketchup may seem harmless enough, over the years it has incited more than a few culture wars. One involved the H. J. Heinz company, which wanted to make a name for itself. A few decades after its founding in 1869, the company decided to break with standard industry practice and side with health-minded reformers who campaigned against the addition of chemical preservatives, especially benzoate, used to keep the bottles from exploding. In 1906 Heinz stopped adding benzoates to their ketchup. At the same time, they amped up the proportions of sugar, vinegar, and spices to yield the now-familiar thick, tartly sweet condiment. Competing ketchup companies responded with a furious lobbying campaign to convince the fledgling Food and Drug Administration of the need for chemicals. But Heinz prevailed, and in so doing they cornered the market and more or less conquered the world. Today the company name is virtually synonymous with ketchup.

Another war was ignited in 1981, when President Ronald Reagan proposed defining ketchup as a vegetable rather than a condiment. This proposal was intended as a cost-saving measure in the nutritional guidelines for federally funded school lunches. The idea of substituting a sugary condiment for a whole-food vegetable quickly came to symbolize the worst of Reaganomics, a policy that deprived those who most need governmental help. The outcry was so vocal that the proposal was killed within a few weeks.

More recently, ketchup battles became international. By the twenty-first century Canada had become the largest importer of American ketchup, but in 2014 Heinz closed its Ontario factory, leading to massive job losses and causing an angry backlash. Into the fray stepped French's, an American company famous for its mustard. French's saw an opportunity to move onto ketchup's turf and began producing the condiment with a bottle featuring a maple leaf on the label and the words "Bottled in Canada with 100% Canadian tomatoes." Sales skyrocketed; Heinz suffered. In 2018 Prime Minister Justin Trudeau placed a 10 percent tariff on American ketchup—largely in response to American tariffs on Canadian aluminum and steel but also due to continuing hostility toward Heinz.

Canada isn't the only member of the British Commonwealth to feel strongly about ketchup. English footballers are also passionate about the condiment. Ketchup wars have periodically erupted in the locker rooms of England's football teams when new managers have peremptorily banished ketchup from the club cafeterias, claiming that the condiment is unhealthy for an elite athlete's diet. Teams have risen up in protest, and a truce is usually reached when a new manager is hired. These battles aren't solely about a cherished condiment, though. Those who want ketchup banned strive for a more disciplined approach to professional athletics, while those who defend ketchup at nearly every meal maintain that its proscription represents a joyless approach to life, one that will ultimately harm the players' emotional health. Ketchup wins out in the end.

Claes Oldenburg, *Ketchup, Thick and Thin*, 1965.

Ketchup

MAKES 2½ CUPS *or* 590 MILLILITERS

Bumper Crop Ketchup

Ever since tomato ketchup became a global favorite, it's been growing sweeter; today's best-selling commercial product is laden with sugar. Our recipe not only brings the condiment back to its savory roots but intensifies the taste of fresh tomatoes by fermenting them, then concentrating them into a paste. Next, we give the cooked, spiced ketchup a further boost by letting it ferment for a few more days before bottling. The result is a truly tomatoey ketchup with a seductive tang.

1½ cups/360 g Fermented Tomato Paste (recipe follows) or 12 ounces/340 g store-bought tomato paste
5 tablespoons/80 ml salt brine, either from homemade lacto-fermented vegetables or from a fermented commercial brand
¼ cup/60 ml apple cider vinegar
¼ cup/60 ml Worcestershire sauce, homemade (page 58) or store bought
3 tablespoons/60 g pure maple syrup
1½ teaspoons kosher salt
¼ teaspoon onion powder
¼ teaspoon ground cayenne pepper
½ teaspoon finely ground black pepper
⅛ teaspoon ground allspice

Place all of the ingredients in the jar of a blender. Purée until smooth. Transfer the ketchup to a nonreactive jar. Place the lid on loosely and let the ketchup ferment at room temperature for 3 to 5 days. Unscrew the lid each day to "burp" the ketchup of any gas that is building up inside the jar, then tighten the lid again. The ketchup is ready once it tastes nicely tangy. Store in the refrigerator for up to 3 months.

SERVING SUGGESTIONS ADD TO THOUSAND ISLAND DRESSING FOR A DEEPER FLAVOR / INCLUDE IN A GLAZE FOR MEATLOAF / MIX 2 TEASPOONS KETCHUP WITH 1 TABLESPOON MAYONNAISE AND 2 TO 3 DASHES HOT SAUCE FOR A "SECRET SAUCE" ON BURGERS AND WINGS

FERMENTED TOMATO PASTE

5 pounds/2.3 kg ripe tomatoes
Kosher salt

Stem and wash the tomatoes. Use a paring knife to remove any bruised spots and cut out the cores.

Use either a food mill or a blender to purée the tomatoes. If using a food mill, core and chop the tomatoes, then run them straight through the mill to purée them and remove their skins and seeds all at once.

If you're using a blender, leave the cored tomatoes intact but cut a small, shallow X in the blossom end. Bring a large pot of water to a boil and set up an ice bath. Drop the tomatoes into the pot, a few at a time, and boil just long enough to loosen their skins, about 15 seconds. (Do not overcook, or you will kill all the good bacteria that aid fermentation.) Using a slotted spoon, transfer the tomatoes to the ice bath to cool. Peel away the skins and, working over a bowl, squeeze out as many of the seeds as possible. Purée the tomatoes in the blender until smooth; if desired, press through a fine-mesh sieve. You should have 2 quarts/2 liters of purée.

Add 1½ percent salt by weight. For 2 quarts/2 liters, this amounts to 3 tablespoons plus 1 teaspoon/30 g. Transfer the mixture to a nonreactive container and wipe down the sides above the purée until they are completely clean. Press a piece of cheesecloth directly on the surface of the purée, where some harmless mold will form as the tomatoes ferment. The cheesecloth will capture the mold and make it easy to remove.

Loosely cover the container with a dish towel to allow the natural yeasts to bloom and place it in a low-light area with an ambient temperature of 60° to 68°F/16° to 20°C to ferment for 3 to 5 days. Check on the purée once a day: remove the cheesecloth, rinse it thoroughly, stir the purée, and reapply the cheesecloth.

After 3 to 5 days, the purée should taste gently sour. If you think it needs more time, continue the process until the tomatoes taste as acidic as you like. Transfer the purée to a 9 by 13-inch/24 by 36 cm Pyrex baking dish and smooth the surface so that the purée is no more than 2 inches/5 cm deep. Dehydrate at 125°F/52°C for 12 to 16 hours (or more, if the tomatoes are watery), until the tomatoes reach the consistency of canned tomato paste, stirring halfway through to prevent a thick skin from forming on top. (If you notice any small, white mold spores, use a clean spoon to carefully remove them; they're harmless.) You should end up with 1½ cups/350 ml of paste. Transfer the paste to a blender or food processor and purée until smooth. If you don't want to use it right away, pack the paste into small jars and refrigerate for up to 1 year.

MAKES 1¼ CUPS *or* 300 MILLILITERS

Mushroom Catsup

In 1876 the H. J. Heinz company introduced their now world-famous condiment as "tomato catsup," a predominantly American spelling of the Indonesian fish sauce known as kecap. *But not long thereafter Heinz changed the branding to "ketchup" to differentiate their product from others, and this spelling eventually stuck.*

Until tomato ketchup took hold, mushroom catsup was extremely popular, and for good reason. Its flavor is rich, deep, and ever so slightly sweet, reminiscent of sweet soy sauce. Use this condiment to heighten the mushroom flavor in your favorite recipes or to perk up any dishes that seem lackluster in taste. We enjoy it in its pure form, drizzled straight over ripe tomatoes and fresh, soft cheese. Don't be surprised by the thin consistency of this catsup, which is typical of condiments by that name that were enjoyed before thick tomato ketchup became a household mainstay.

2½ pounds/1.13 kg button mushrooms, stems trimmed
2 teaspoons kosher salt
1½ ounces/43 g dried porcini mushrooms
4 cups/950 ml hot water
2 sheets dried kombu, each 3 by 6 inches/7.5 by 15 cm
1 medium onion, thinly sliced
4 large garlic cloves, coarsely chopped
1 tablespoon fresh thyme leaves
1 tablespoon black peppercorns
1 teaspoon coriander seed
¼ teaspoon dried red pepper flakes
⅛ teaspoon celery seed
⅛ teaspoon anise seed
1 large bay leaf
1 whole clove
¼ cup/60 ml malt vinegar
3 tablespoons/45 ml Worcestershire sauce, homemade (page 58) or store bought
1 firmly packed tablespoon dark brown sugar

Preheat the oven to a very low setting (about 160°F/70°C). Working in batches, pulse the button mushrooms in a food processor until they are thoroughly minced, but not so far that they become a homogeneous paste. You may also grate them using the processor's shredding disc. Transfer the mushrooms to a deep, stainless-steel baking pan (ideally 9 by 3 by 4 inches/24 by 36 by 10 cm), spread them in an even layer, and mix in the salt. Leave at least 2 inches of headspace from the top of the mushrooms to the rim of the pan. Cover the pan with a layer of plastic wrap and then a layer of aluminum foil. (Don't be concerned about using plastic wrap at this low temperature; it really helps the mushrooms to steam.) Place the pan in the oven and bake until the mushrooms have released all their liquid, about 12 hours.

Remove the pan from the oven and carefully open the plastic wrap and foil. Strain the broth through a fine-mesh sieve into a deep stainless-steel or enameled cast-iron pot, pressing hard on the solids, which will look like dry, dull brown duxelles when you're done. You should end up with about 3¼ cups/800 ml of mushroom liquid. Discard the solids. CONTINUED ▸

MUSHROOM CATSUP CONTINUED

In a medium bowl, soak the porcini in the hot water for 30 minutes, until softened. Strain the porcini liquid into the mushroom liquid, pressing down on the solids. You should have about 7 cups/1.65 L of combined broths. (Save the porcini for another use.)

Add the kombu to the mushroom broth and let it soak until it begins to soften, about 2 hours. Then place the pot over medium heat, bring the liquid to a gentle simmer, and stir in the onion, garlic, thyme, peppercorns, coriander seed, red pepper flakes, celery seed, anise seed, bay leaf, and clove. Cook, covered, at a gentle simmer for 1 hour. The kombu should be tender enough to pierce with a chopstick.

Strain the broth through a fine-mesh sieve into a large, heavy saucepan. Stir in the malt vinegar, Worcestershire sauce, and brown sugar. Cook, uncovered, over very low heat, stirring occasionally, until the liquid has reduced to 1¼ cups/300 ml; this will take 2 to 3 hours. Let the catsup cool completely, then transfer it to a nonreactive, airtight container. Once cool, the catsup can be used immediately. Store it in the refrigerator for up to 1 year.

SERVING SUGGESTIONS USE IN DRESSINGS TO ADD UMAMI / DRIZZLE OVER TOMATOES AND BURRATA CHEESE / ADD TO MUSHROOM DISHES TO INTENSIFY THEIR FLAVOR / STIR A LITTLE INTO GROUND BEEF FOR A SUCCULENT HAMBURGER

MAKES ¾ CUP *or* 175 MILLILITERS

Black Salt

On the Thursday before Easter, Russians historically prepared a charred black salt that was believed to purify the body and soul at the advent of spring. They continued to prize this special salt throughout the year both for the excellent flavor it confers and for its health benefits. The regular consumption of a little salt dissolved in a glass of water was said to keep illness at bay—a good thing in remote villages where doctors might be hundreds of versts away.

Black salt is also an example of Russian resourcefulness. Its traditional base is the sediment left over from making kvass, the slightly alcoholic drink itself made from leftover black bread. But if time is short, or if you don't have kvass sediment on hand, black salt can be quickly prepared with fresh rye bread, or even with rye flour, and some versions even call for oats instead of rye. The recipe here is made especially flavorful from the addition of kombu, a seaweed also known as laminaria or kelp, which grows prolifically along the Arctic coast. It is healthful, too, thanks to kombu's high levels of iodine, iron, and potassium.

3 by 6-inch/7.5 by 15 cm sheet kombu
⅓ cup/10 g small torn pieces of unseeded rye bread
¼ cup/70 g coarse sea salt
½ teaspoon dill seed
½ teaspoon coriander seed

Soak the kombu in 2 cups/475 ml water overnight.

The next day, drain the kombu, reserving the water. Finely chop the kombu and set aside.

In a small bowl, soak the bread in ½ cup/125 ml of the kombu water to cover for 30 minutes, until it has absorbed enough water to become very moist. Drain off the excess water but don't press down on the solids. Return the moistened bread to the bowl and stir in the sea salt, dill seed, coriander seed, and chopped kombu, mixing well.

Preheat the oven to 500°F/260°C. Grease a small cast-iron skillet with a light film of vegetable oil.

Shape the bread and salt mixture into a 4-inch/10 cm disk and place it in the pan.

Bake at 500°F for 30 minutes, until the disk is hard and charred. Carefully remove the pan from the oven. You'll encounter a whoosh of smoke when you open the oven door. If you can, take the smoking pan right outside to let it cool.

When the disk has cooled, lift it from the pan and place it in an unbreakable bowl or pan with deep sides. Break the disk into chunks with a mallet or meat tenderizer.

Transfer the chunks to a mini food processor and grind to your preference, from medium-fine to fine. The salt can be used immediately. Stored airtight, it keeps indefinitely.

SERVING SUGGESTIONS USE AS A FINISHING SALT ON ALL KINDS OF MEATS, STEAMED OR GRILLED VEGETABLES, AND FISH / ADD TO MARINADES, SOUPS, AND STEWS / MIX WITH SEEDS TO TOP HOMEMADE BAGELS OR BREAD BEFORE BAKING

BANCHAN

Banchan is a loosely defined category of side dishes in Korean cuisine. It includes preserved and pickled vegetables, salted fish, fish guts or roe, boiled meats, tofu or tofu skin, egg casseroles, and stews, along with a seemingly limitless variety of kimchi. Banchan is really anything that you eat with *bap*, the ubiquitous bowl of steamed rice that accompanies every meal in Korea. To understand banchan, you have to go back nearly two thousand years to the Three Kingdoms period, when Buddhism was the predominant religion and meals consisted mainly of vegetables and rice. Nowadays, we may think of barbecued pork or beef as a staple of the Korean diet, but this emphasis on meat represents a modern shift. The core of Korea's culinary identity has always been vegetables, including the fermented condiments that characterize the deep flavors of banchan.

At home, banchan can be as modest as a cabbage kimchi, a handful of dried seaweed sheets, and pickled daikon radish. Special meals are celebrated by offering an array of Hansik banchan—traditional Korean foods—served in tranquil celadon bowls. Restaurants in Korea are often rated on the quality and variety of their banchan. A typical banchan offering will include a cabbage kimchi, a radish or cucumber kimchi, dried baby anchovies, marinated mung bean sprouts, marinated spinach in sesame oil, perhaps a preserved root vegetable like lotus or bellflower root, marinated raw crab, boiled beef in sweet soy sauce, and sometimes a steaming dish of egg custard served in a stone crock. Depending on the restaurant, you may also see banchan potato salad or even Spam, variations that are remnants of American influence during the Korean War. They demonstrate not banchan's cultural absorption but its ever-changing philosophy.

Although banchan are not meant to be the main component of the meal, I have spent many an evening enjoying nothing but a bowl of rice and a few helpings of salty and sour banchan. The key to banchan is that each small dish is simple, intensely flavored, and made in advance, so that it can be served at a moment's notice.

When I was a child and a family friend would come to the house unannounced, my grandmother would quickly fix a meal with a bowl of rice and an array of preserved and pickled vegetables, which were waiting in glass jars in our fridge. Such a meal was humble but also delicious and, most importantly, a way to welcome visitors. That is the real purpose of banchan, to nurture and to comfort. It is less a food than a language, one that most Koreans learn alongside their first words. The vocabulary of banchan conveys the beauty and joy and love of a cuisine that has endured over thousands of years.

EDWARD LEE
Chef and author, Louisville, Kentucky and Washington, DC

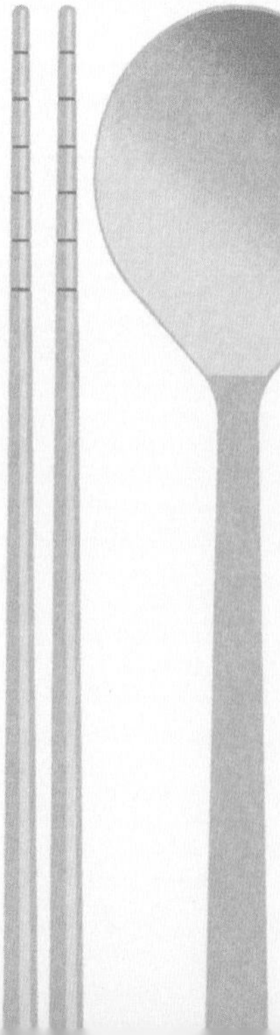

Poggi Kimchi

Korea boasts a good two hundred varieties of kimchi, made from all sorts of vegetables and in many different styles. Even the familiar Napa cabbage kimchi, known as baechu, *comes in two styles: the chopped* mak *you regularly find at the grocery store and the whole-leaf* poggi *we offer here. Poggi kimchi is the more flavorful and aesthetically pleasing of the two, with its leaves shaped into neat bundles.*

Kimchi lovers are divided between those who like their condiment fresh, after only a few days of fermentation, and those who appreciate the intensity of aged kimchi. As the kimchi ferments and ages, the strong flavors of the seafood—dried salted shrimp, fish sauce, and smoked oysters in our version—evolve, and what starts out as a crisp, lively version of the classic Korean condiment eventually turns deeply funky. Korean cooks agree that fresh poggi is best served with rice or as a refreshing banchan; when aged, it becomes an excellent addition to stews, soups, or fried rice.

Korean kimchi is fermented in porous clay pots called onggi. *Traditionally these pots were buried underground in the winter to keep the kimchi from freezing. These days, most families have a special "kimchi refrigerator" where they can store any number of ferments to ensure that there will always be a ready supply of these healthful and flavorful preparations.*

CABBAGE

1 Napa cabbage (about 2 pounds/900 g), quartered lengthwise with root ends left intact
6 tablespoons/54 g kosher salt

RICE FLOUR PASTE

3½ tablespoons/55 ml vegetable stock
1½ teaspoons sweet (glutinous) rice flour

SEASONING PASTE

1 tablespoon/5 g dried salted shrimp
1½ ounces/45 g smoked oysters in oil, drained
2 tablespoons/30 ml unsweetened fish sauce, such as Red Boat
2 tablespoons/30 ml vegetable stock
4 teaspoons minced garlic
2¼ teaspoons peeled and finely grated fresh ginger
1 teaspoon coconut sugar or granulated sugar
6 tablespoons/33 g gochugaru (Korean chile flakes)
⅓ cup (35 g) thinly sliced yellow onion
2 green onions, green parts only, cut into 2-inch/5 cm pieces
½ small, tart apple, such as Pink Lady or Granny Smith, or a small Asian pear, peeled and grated
3 tablespoons/3 g Chinese chives, cut into 2-inch/5 cm pieces

PREPARE THE CABBAGE: Rinse the cabbage quarters under cold running water and place on a large, rimmed sheet pan. Generously salt the cabbage all over, making sure to season between the leaves as well as on the surface. (Don't worry about being too precise since the cabbage will shed water and the salt will distribute evenly into the brine.) Set aside to brine at room temperature, cut-sides up, until the hard leaves become limp and soggy, about 4 hours, flipping once or twice. If the leaves haven't softened sufficiently, let them soak for another hour or so. The cabbage quarters should release plenty of water into the pan.

MAKE THE RICE FLOUR PASTE: When the cabbages are brined and ready to process, prepare an ice bath. In a small saucepan, bring 2 tablespoons/30 ml of the vegetable stock to a boil. In a measuring cup, combine the sweet rice flour with the remaining 1½ tablespoons/25 ml of stock. Whisk this mixture into the boiling stock and stir for 15 seconds until the mixture is very thick. Remove from the heat and set the pan in the ice bath to cool the paste to room temperature, stirring occasionally, for 5 to 10 minutes.

MAKE THE SEASONING PASTE: In a food processor fitted with a metal blade, combine the dried shrimp, oysters, fish sauce, vegetable stock, garlic, ginger, coconut sugar, and the rice flour paste. Purée. Transfer the mixture to a bowl and add 2 tablespoons/11 g of the gochugaru chile flakes and mix well. Let the seasoning paste sit for 15 minutes to allow the flavors to meld.

Rinse the salted cabbage quarters under cold running water, squeezing out the excess liquid with your hands. Set aside.

In a large bowl, toss the onion, green onions, apple, and Chinese chives with the remaining 4 tablespoons/22 g gochugaru chile flakes until the chile flakes lightly coat the vegetables. Add the seasoning paste and mix until evenly distributed.

Place one cabbage quarter in the bowl with the seasoning sauce. With clean hands, slather one-quarter of the sauce all over the outsides and between each leaf, tucking in the larger pieces of green onion and apple as well. Fold the cabbage quarter in half crosswise, gathering the leafy tail ends together and bringing them up and over the root end to create a compact bundle. Place the bundle in a sterilized 1-gallon/4 L crock. Repeat with the remaining cabbage quarters until you have used up most of the sauce and the crock is filled with sauced cabbage, with about 1 inch/2.5 cm of headspace at the top. (Don't worry if there are a few air pockets; they'll fill with liquid as the kimchi ferments.) Top the crock with any remaining sauce.

Lay a piece of parchment paper or plastic wrap over the cabbage bundles and place a heavy weight on the top, then loosely cover the crock with a lid. As the cabbage ferments, it will expand, so be sure to place the crock on a plate or in a bowl to catch the overflow. Leave for 2 to 7 days, tasting each day to test the degree of sourness. When the kimchi is to your liking, transfer it to the refrigerator, where it will keep for at least 3 months.

To serve, present the cabbage whole for dramatic effect or cut it into 1-inch/2.5 cm slices.

SERVING SUGGESTIONS STUFF INDIVIDUAL LEAVES WITH GROUND PORK AND BAKE / CHOP INTO STEWS / SERVE ALONGSIDE GRILLED MEATS AND RICE

Sweet and Sour Pickled Mushrooms

Quick-pickled mushrooms are a mainstay of the Asian larder: a handy side dish for rice or a lively addition to stir-fries. Often the mushrooms are used within a few hours, but we let ours sit overnight before serving to enhance their flavor. This Korean-style pickle will last in the fridge up to a month, its flavor continually improving as the soy sauce and gochugaru flakes infuse the mushrooms with umami and heat. Rice vinegar adds a gentle acidity, while brown sesame seeds lend earthiness. The green onions, garlic, and ginger all provide welcome crunch. So good is this pickle that when the flavors are at their peak, these mushrooms might just steal the show as part of a banchan or composed dish.

MUSHROOMS

½ cup/120 ml toasted sesame oil
1 pound/454 g baby shiitake mushrooms, stemmed (or large shiitake, stemmed and cut into ¼-inch/6 mm slices or quartered)

MARINADE

½ cup/120 ml soy sauce
3½ tablespoons/55 ml unseasoned rice vinegar
3 tablespoons/36 g sucanat (unrefined cane sugar) or light brown sugar
1½-inch/3.75 cm piece fresh ginger, peeled and finely minced
2 small garlic cloves, finely minced
3 green onions, green and white parts, sliced into thin rings
3½ tablespoons/31.5 g brown sesame seeds
2½ tablespoons /14 g gochugaru (Korean chile flakes)
1 teaspoon kosher salt

MAKE THE MUSHROOMS: Warm a medium sauté pan over medium heat, then add the sesame oil and heat until shimmering. Add the mushrooms and sauté until they just begin to soften and glisten, 3 to 4 minutes. Set aside to cool to room temperature.

MAKE THE MARINADE: In a 1-pint/475 ml jar, combine the soy sauce, rice vinegar, sucanat, ginger, garlic, green onions, sesame seeds, gochugaru, and salt. Stir until the sucanat dissolves.

Stir the cooled mushrooms into the marinade, mixing well. Allow them to sit at room temperature for 8 hours or overnight before transferring to the refrigerator. They will keep, refrigerated, for 1 month; the flavor will continue to improve.

SERVING SUGGESTIONS ADD TO CHEESE AND CHARCUTERIE BOARDS / TOSS WITH ROASTED WILD MUSHROOMS / SERVE WITH GRILLED MEATS AND RICE

Gochujang

This Korean chile paste, known for its bright red hue and addictive interplay of sweet, savory, and spicy flavors, has become a staple in many American kitchens. But we know little of its long history in Korea. Red peppers arrived in Asia from the Americas in the sixteenth century, evolving into Chinese and fiery Thai peppers with higher Scoville units of heat. But the milder red pepper known as gochu, *which forms the base of gochujang, is likely a different variety native to Korea, since the use of gochu in Korean fermentation practices, such as the making of kimchi, has been documented as long as 1,500 years ago—more than 1,000 years before the arrival of the American pepper. Gochujang itself probably originated around the same time. Early texts reveal that it was initially considered a medicinal food, used to improve digestion, long before becoming the popular condiment that it is today.*

Gochujang's base consists of sweet rice flour, malt barley, fermented soybean flour, and powdered gochugaru (Korean red chile), with a little rice syrup added for sweetening. Because the process of making it is so involved, most of the gochujang eaten today is commercially prepared, even in South Korea. So why, you might ask, make gochujang from scratch? Beyond the satisfaction of reenacting a centuries-old tradition of long fermentation, homemade gochujang bestows health benefits. The peppers are rich in capsaicin, which speeds up the metabolism and helps to burn fat, while the fermentation process yields gut-friendly probiotics.

2¼ cups/245 g barley malt flakes (yeotgireum)
9 cups/2.16 liters warm water
1¼ cups/250 g sweet rice flour (such as Mochiko)
½ cup plus 1 Tbsp/140 g fine sea salt, plus more for sprinkling
1½ cups/125 g fermented soybean powder (mejugaru)
2 cups/300 g fine Korean red chile powder (gochugaru), not flakes
12 garlic cloves, peeled and microplaned
½ cup/120 ml rice syrup

Put the barley malt in a large bowl. Stir in 5 cups/1.2 L of the warm water and let the mixture sit overnight at room temperature.

The next day, gently pulse the malt and the water in batches in a blender to produce a very milky liquid, taking care not to emulsify the mixture into a paste. Set a fine sieve or cheesecloth-lined strainer over a large, heavy pot and strain the malt liquid through it. Gently press on the malt husks with the back of a spoon or squeeze the cheesecloth with your hands to extract the remaining liquid.

Return the malt husks to the first bowl and add the remaining 4 cups/.96 L of water. Rub the husks between your palms to extract the rest of the milky liquid. Strain this liquid into the pot with the first batch. You should have 8 to 9 cups/1. 9 to 2 L of malt water. Discard the residual malt solids.

Add the sweet rice flour to the malt water, whisking to ensure that no clumps form. Place the pot over low heat and gently warm the liquid to 100° F/38° C, stirring well. Remove the pot from the heat and leave to sit for 3 hours. This rest period allows time for the enzymes in the malt to convert the complex starches in the rice powder to simple sugars.

Place the pot over medium heat and bring the liquid to a boil; cook until it has reduced to 4½ cups/1 L. Remove 1 cup/250 ml of the liquid from the pot and set it aside to thin the paste later, if necessary.

Add the salt to the liquid remaining in the pot and stir to dissolve. Whisk in the fermented soybean powder, mixing well. If clumps form, give the mixture a quick blitz with an immersion blender. Repeat with the red chile powder, garlic, and rice syrup. Continue to stir the mixture, now using a large wooden spoon or spatula. At this point the gochujang should be like thick muffin batter. If it is too thick, add reserved malt liquid as necessary.

Let the mixture sit for a few hours until all of the liquid has been absorbed and the salt has completely dissolved. The gochujang will taste too salty at this point but will mellow during fermentation. Transfer it to a jar or small earthenware vessel such as a traditional onggi, if you have one. Lightly dust the top with fine sea salt. Place a piece of cheesecloth or plastic wrap directly on the surface to inhibit the growth of mold.

Place the lid on. Ferment the gochujang indoors at room temperature (65 to 72°F/18 to 22°C). On sunny days, place the jar outside and remove the lid to allow some exposure to sunlight. This small batch takes approximately 90 days to ferment. Once it is done, refrigerate the gochujang in a sealed container. It will keep for a year or more.

SERVING SUGGESTIONS USE AS A MARINADE FOR CHICKEN AND BEEF / SPICE UP SOUPS AND STEWS WITH IT / SERVE WITH FRIED CHICKEN OR HAMBURGERS / MIX WITH WATER, SESAME OIL, SAKE, RICE VINEGAR, OR SOY SAUCE FOR A DIPPING SAUCE

MAKES ABOUT 1½ QUARTS *or* 1.4 LITERS

Mostarda di Frutta

*Italian mostarda is a heady condiment, a more interesting addition to a charcuterie board than quince paste or fig spread. This sweet-and-sour medley is traditionally prepared by candying various fruits in concentrated grape must over several days, then adding a savory touch with mustard—though the condiment's name derives not from the mustard (*senape *in Italian) but from the must (Latin* musto*). A specialty of Cremona in northern Italy, this vibrant relish can be traced back to the ancient Roman practice of preserving fruits and vegetables in vinegar and honey. Our simplified recipe produces a delectable relish in under two hours.*

4 cups/950 ml dry white wine
1¼ cups/170 g sucanat (unrefined cane sugar) or 220 g light brown sugar
¼ cup/60 ml white balsamic vinegar
2 large green apples (about 1 pound/454 g), such as Granny Smith, peeled, cored, and cut into ½-inch/1.25 cm cubes
6 ounces/170 g dried apricots, quartered
6 ounces/170 g dried apples, finely diced
4 ounces/110 g dried pitted sour cherries, halved
2 shallots, minced
3 tablespoons/47 g Dijon mustard
2 tablespoons/22 g yellow mustard seed
1 tablespoon minced fresh lemon thyme or thyme
2 bay leaves
Zest of 1 lemon
Zest of ½ orange
½ teaspoon kosher salt, or to taste
¼ teaspoon cayenne pepper

Bring all of the ingredients to a boil in a 4-quart/4 L saucepan over medium-high heat. Decrease the heat and cook the mixture over low heat, stirring frequently, until the apricots and cherries are plumped, the apples have broken down, and the liquid is reduced and thickened, about 30 minutes. Cool to room temperature, then remove the bay leaves. Taste for seasoning, adding more salt if desired. Serve right away or transfer to an airtight jar and store in the refrigerator for up to 1 month.

SERVING SUGGESTIONS USE ON A CHARCUTERIE AND CHEESE BOARD / SERVE ALONGSIDE ROASTED OR GRILLED GAME, OR WITH SAUSAGES / MIX INTO GREEK YOGURT AND SERVE WITH LAMB

MAKES 2½ CUPS *or* 600 MILLILITERS

Salsa Macha with Pickled Peanuts

Here's a salsa that calls for nary a tomato or tomatillo. But then many Mexican salsas defy expectations and remain known only locally. Salsa macha, an oil-based condiment that relies on dried chiles for flavor, was one of the obscure ones until recently, when the New York Times *named it "the most valuable condiment of 2020." This salsa hails from the coastal state of Veracruz, where the cuisine absorbed many cross-cultural currents. Salsa macha shows traces of ancient, indigenous Mesoamerican practice in the use of dried chiles and pumpkin seeds, but the impact of the Spanish conquest is clear from its generous amounts of oil and garlic. Meanwhile, peanuts betray a West African influence. Our recipe calls for pickled peanuts to add an extra zing. Though salsa macha isn't hard to make, you want to be sure to keep the chiles and garlic from burning, lest they turn bitter.*

The finished salsa separates on standing, which is actually a benefit, allowing you to use it two ways: stir it together for a chunky topping or simply spoon off some of the flavored oil from the top to use as a spicy finishing sauce. We would love this salsa for its name alone: macha *is the feminine form of macho, hence "She-Man Sauce," in Zarela Martinez's playful translation. But the multidimensional flavor is what truly enchants us. Thanks to the preservative effects of oil, salsa macha lasts a couple of months without spoiling—but that applies only if you can resist eating it up right away.*

PICKLED PEANUTS

6 ounces / 170 g raw peanuts in the shell
2 tablespoons / 18 g, plus ¼ cup / 36 g kosher salt
1 chile de árbol
1½ tablespoons coriander seed, toasted
1 teaspoon dried oregano
1 whole head garlic, cut straight through horizontally
2 cups / 475 ml apple cider vinegar
Scant ½ cup / 100 g sugar

SALSA MACHA

1 heaping cup / 170 g drained pickled peanuts
1 cup / 240 ml peanut oil
½ cup / 120 ml grapeseed oil
½ cup / 120 ml olive oil
6 ancho chiles, stemmed, seeded, and sliced into ½-inch / 1.25 cm strips
6 guajillo chiles, stemmed, seeded, and sliced into ½-inch / 1.25 cm strips
3 chiles de árbol, stemmed, seeded, and sliced into ½-inch / 1.25 cm strips
2 tablespoons / 17 g pumpkin seeds
1 tablespoon black sesame seeds
5 garlic cloves, finely minced
3 tablespoons / 45 ml peanut pickling liquid
1 teaspoon dried marjoram or Mexican oregano
1 teaspoon coriander seed, toasted and ground
Zest of 1 lime
Salt

MAKE THE PICKLED PEANUTS: Combine the peanuts, 2 tablespoons / 18 g salt, chile, coriander, oregano, and garlic in a large pot. Pour in enough water to cover the peanuts when you push them down with a spoon. Cover and bring to a boil. Stir, then lower the heat to a gentle simmer. Cover and cook until the nuts have the texture of cooked chickpeas, 2 to 4 hours, depending on how fresh the peanuts are. Check the water level every hour, adding warm tap water if it gets too low. CONTINUED ▸

SALSA MACHA WITH PICKLED PEANUTS CONTINUED

When the peanuts are ready, remove the pot from the heat and allow the peanuts to cool in the liquid. Then strain them, discarding the boiling liquid. Shell the nuts and transfer them to a 1-pint/475 ml canning jar.

In a small saucepan, combine the vinegar, sugar, and ¼ cup/36 g salt and bring to a boil. Remove the pan from the heat and allow the brine to sit for 5 minutes. Carefully pour the brine over the peanuts. When cool, cover the jar with a tight-fitting lid and refrigerate for at least 1 week before using. Pickled peanuts will keep for 6 months in the refrigerator.

MAKE THE SALSA: Preheat the oven to 325°F/160°C.

With a slotted spoon, lift the pickled peanuts from the brine and place them on a baking pan. Remove any remaining skins by pressing down on the nuts to break them in half if they haven't already naturally separated. Toast for 10 to 12 minutes, until the peanuts begin to take on color.

In a large Dutch oven or other heavy, high-walled pot, heat the peanut, grapeseed, and olive oils to 325°F/160°C. Gently fry the ancho chiles, guajillo chiles, and chiles de árbol until they have puffed up, 5 to 7 minutes. With a slotted spoon, transfer them to a bowl.

Carefully add the peanuts to the oil (have a lid handy in case they spatter) and fry them for a minute or two until golden brown; transfer them with a slotted spoon to the bowl with the chiles. Add the pumpkin and sesame seeds to the oil and fry for 2 to 3 minutes, just until they begin to take on color. Remove the pot from the heat and add the garlic, frying only until it is golden but not burnt. Then return the chiles and peanuts to the oil.

Carefully add the 3 tablespoons of pickling liquid and allow the mixture to cool for 5 minutes before stirring in the marjoram, coriander seed, and lime zest. Cool to body temperature.

With a slotted spoon, transfer the larger solids like the peanuts and chiles to a food processor and pulse a few times to break them up. Add the rest of the mixture, including the frying oil, and pulse gently until all of the pieces are about the size of sesame seeds. The texture should remain crunchy. Season with salt to taste and spoon it into small jars. The salsa macha can be eaten immediately. It will keep in the refrigerator for up to 2 months.

SERVING SUGGESTIONS SPOON OVER FRIED EGGS / TOSS WITH ROASTED VEGETABLES / MIX INTO FRIED RICE / USE AS A DIP FOR CHICKEN WINGS

MAKES 1 QUART *or* 1 LITER

Pikliz

Haitians serve this pickled slaw along with griot and plantains, brilliantly playing up the contrast of colors and textures, and balancing the fat of the fried pork with acidity and heat from the scotch bonnet peppers. We find that its brightness plays well with stir-fries, tacos, and more.

The condiment's name—pronounced peek-leez—reflects the French colonization of Haiti, drawing from the word piquer *(to sting), an apt root. Although pikliz looks like coleslaw, it is in fact very spicy and vinegary, so it's best served directly on food, not on the side. Pikliz has migrated around the world with the Haitian diaspora, becoming a versatile condiment to offset fattiness while pumping up the flavor and heat.*

2 cups/115 g thinly sliced green cabbage
1 small red or green bell pepper, stemmed, seeded, and thinly sliced
1 large red onion, thinly sliced
1 large carrot, peeled and shaved into long strips with a peeler
3 green onions, green and white parts, sliced into ¼-inch/6 mm rounds
1 to 2 scotch bonnet peppers (depending on desired spiciness), finely minced (remove seeds if less heat is desired)
2 garlic cloves, finely minced
10 whole black peppercorns
4 whole allspice berries
2 teaspoons thyme leaves stripped from the stems
1 sprig marjoram
2 teaspoons kosher salt
3 cups/720 ml apple cider vinegar or champagne vinegar
Juice of 1 lime

In a large bowl, combine the cabbage, bell pepper, red onion, carrot, green onions, scotch bonnet peppers, garlic cloves, peppercorns, allspice berries, thyme, marjoram, and salt.

Toss well to combine. Pack the mixture tightly into a 1-quart/950 ml jar. Stir the vinegar and lime juice together and pour over the vegetables. Press down on the vegetables until they are completely submerged in the liquid. Tightly cover the jar with a lid and refrigerate for at least 3 days before opening. Pikliz will last up to 3 months, refrigerated.

SERVING SUGGESTIONS SERVE ALONGSIDE FATTY CUTS OF MEAT LIKE PORK BELLY, OR WITH WHOLE ROASTED CHICKEN / FINELY CHOP AND ADD TO COLESLAW OR STIR-FRIES / SAUTÉ IN PORK OR CHICKEN FAT AND SERVE ON TOP OF GRILLED VEGETABLES / TUCK INTO TACOS

Tamarind Concentrate

NOTES ON CANNING

Preserves can be processed in a water bath for longer-term storage. Use sturdy glass canning jars with two-piece lids—a flat lid with rubber edges and a metal ring. Before filling the jars, sterilize them by placing them on a rack in a canning pot or large stockpot. Cover the jars with hot water, place a lid on the pot, and bring to a boil. Boil for 10 minutes. Place the jar lids and other utensils you plan to use in a separate smaller pot and simmer for 10 minutes. The jars and lids can remain in the water until you're ready to use them, as long as they remain hot.

Use tongs to lift the jars from the pot and pour out the water. Set the jars upright on a kitchen towel on the counter. Working quickly, fill the jars to the top with your preserves, leaving ½ inch / 1.3 cm of headspace, as ingredients can expand during the canning process. With a paper towel, carefully wipe away any preserves that might have spilled onto the rim. If any air bubbles have formed, run a blunt knife around the edges of the jar to remove them. Immediately cover each jar with a lid and screw on a metal ring to hold the lid in place during the canning process.

The timing will vary based on the ingredients and equipment you are using. Once you have boiled or steamed your filled jars, promptly and carefully remove them from the boiling water and place them back on the towel-lined countertop to cool.

As the jars cool you will begin to hear a popping sound from time to time; this is the jar sealing. It can take up to 12 hours for jars to seal; you can assist in this process by pressing down on the middle of the lid with your finger, but if the lid does not remain concave it is a faulty seal. If the jars fail to seal, you should re-process the preserves. Depending on the brand of canning pot that you use, the guidelines differ slightly, so be sure to follow the manufacturer's instructions.

Once fully sealed, remove the rings for long-term storage; they are necessary only to hold the lids in place during processing and then again after you open the jar to use the contents. If left on during storage it becomes harder to detect a faulty seal, and the rings can also hold moisture from the canning process and cause rust to form around the edges.

NOTES ON INGREDIENTS

DRIED ANGELINO PLUMS These plums, available online, are a vibrant shade of red. Regular dried plums or apricots can be substituted for a slightly different taste.

DRIED CHILES Chiles have many different flavor profiles. In addition to standard grocery-store crushed red pepper flakes, we favor Mexican chiles such as ancho, guajillo, and chile de árbol, which range in flavor from mild to hot. Aleppo and Urfa peppers have a smoky flavor. The Korean pepper known as gochugaru is sold as both flakes and powder; be sure to use whichever one the recipes specify. Specialty dried chiles are widely available at Latino and Asian markets as well as online.

FERMENTED SOYBEANS The fermented, salted black soybeans known as douchi are available in Asian markets and online. We especially like Yang Jiang Preserved Beans with Ginger.

HONEY Raw, unpasteurized honey is always our first choice, since it retains the healthful properties that are lost when heated.

MAPLE SYRUP We prefer dark grade B syrup for its rich flavor.

SALT Unless otherwise specified, we use Diamond Crystal Kosher Salt in our recipes.

SORGHUM SYRUP Processed from sorghum grain, this syrup is less viscous and slightly less sweet than molasses, a byproduct of sugar refining.

SUGAR Some of our recipes call for sucanat, which is unrefined cane sugar. You can substitute regular granulated sugar, though the taste will be sweeter.

SWEET RICE FLOUR This type of rice flour, usually used as a thickener in Asian cuisines, is made from short-grain rice. It is sometimes called "glutinous rice flour." Regular rice flour is made from medium- and long-grain varieties of rice. The two types are not interchangeable.

VEGETABLE OILS Many recipes call for a neutral vegetable oil. We're partial to grapeseed oil, but a mild sunflower or peanut oil can be used instead. Unless it is specified, olive oil has too distinctive a flavor for most of our recipes.

VINEGAR We use many different types of vinegar, which vary from mild to bold. The gentlest is rice vinegar, which should be unseasoned. For apple cider vinegar, we prefer Bragg organic vinegar. We also use white, champagne, red, and balsamic vinegars made from grapes, as well as distilled white and malt vinegar, the two boldest of all.

NOTES ON EQUIPMENT

BLENDERS Countertop and immersion blenders are put to use in many of the recipes in this book. In some cases, a food processor can be substituted, though blenders can be more effective for puréeing and pulsing certain ingredients.

CANNING JARS Many preservation recipes require a 1-pint/½ L glass canning jar with a metal lid for pickling, fermentation, and storage. It can be handy to have ½-pint or 2-pint jars as well. It's best to stock up on these before starting projects; packages of 6, 12, and 24 jars are usually available.

CHEESECLOTH Used for straining as well as to aerate during fermentation, cheesecloth is essential to have on hand for preservation recipes.

DEHYDRATOR A countertop dehydrator frees up oven or smart-oven space, especially when a recipe calls for 24 hours of slow drying at a very low temperature. Many models come fitted with special trays for dehydrating fruits, vegetables, and herbs.

FERMENTATION CROCKS While jars and glass bowls will usually suffice, contemporary crocks come specially designed for fermenting cabbage and other vegetables and fruits, and can include accessories such as weights and tampers. Korean earthenware crocks, known as *onggi*, are more traditional and are often decorative as well.

FERMENTATION WEIGHTS Glass fermentation weights are used to keep fruits and vegetables submerged in liquids. Substitutes include a clean stone, a small glass dish, or a zip-top bag filled with water.

FINE-MESH SIEVE A well-made fine-mesh sieve is essential for straining, especially when a recipe calls for pressing on solids to extract liquid.

FOOD PROCESSOR For recipes that call for shredding, pulsing, and grinding, it pays to have a good food processor within reach, especially one with multiple blade options. A processor can also be used in place of a blender when necessary.

HEAVY-BOTTOMED, NONREACTIVE PANS Some preservation recipes call for a long, slow simmer. A sturdy stainless-steel pan will keep vegetables and fruits from scorching.

KITCHEN SCALE As with baking, preservation recipes work best when the proportions are strictly followed. Weighing ingredients on a kitchen scale ensures consistency and success.

PARCHMENT PAPER This smooth, greaseproof paper, known for its use in baking and cooking, also plays a key part in preservation recipes that call for fermenting in a jar or crock. Placed directly on top of the ingredients, it will prevent any stray bits from floating to the top, which can cause them to mold when exposed to air.

SPICE GRINDER Because many of our recipes call for grinding whole spices, this affordable electric countertop device is a great time-saver. Grinding by hand in a mortar and pestle is more old-school and tactile, but either method is completely acceptable.

INDEX

ACKNOWLEDGMENTS

DARRA GOLDSTEIN

Thanks first to Cortney and Richard, my friends and coauthors. We enjoyed a dream team for this series, helmed by our visionary editor, Jenny Wapner, with whom it's always a joy to work. I'm also thrilled to be working again with another dear friend, designer Frances Baca, who has brought the books to such vivid life. It was great fun working with photographer David Malosh, whose gorgeous photos grace these books, and prop stylist Ayesha Patel. Thanks, too, to my agent, Angela Miller, and to Carolyn Insley for guiding the books through production. And finally I'm grateful for the unfailing support of my sister, Ardath Weaver, and that of my husband, Dean Crawford—for his math genius, his editing, and his endless enthusiasm for new tastes.

CORTNEY BURNS

In gratitude for the time honored preservation traditions that inspire and enliven our creativity. Thanks to my family for putting up with the plethora of jars and experiments that line our kitchen, and for tasting new and different flavors with wonderment and surprise. To my amazing collaboration team, Darra & Richard; what fun it is to create with you both. And to all the microbes that make this possible; we humbly thank you!

RICHARD MARTIN

I would like to thank my wife, Sonja, and children Apolline and Loic, for taste testing and allowing my food preservation experiments to take over the kitchen for long stretches of time. Thanks also to my extended family: Jan and John, Lee and Lisa, and Greg and Patty. Over the years, as a website and magazine editor, I've worked with many inspiring chefs, writers, and friends who expanded my culinary world—thanks to all of you. And to Darra and Cortney, thank you for developing these incredible recipes and allowing us to share them with the world.

Hardie Grant North America
2912 Telegraph Ave
Berkeley, CA 94705
hardiegrantbooks.com

Published in the United States by Hardie Grant North America, an imprint of Hardie Grant Publishing Pty Ltd.

Library of Congress Cataloging-in-Publication Data is available upon request

ISBN: 9781958417218
ISBN: 9781958417225 (eBook)

Printed in China
Design by Frances Baca
Prop styling by Ayesha Patel

FIRST EDITION

Hardie Grant
NORTH AMERICA

MIX
Paper | Supporting responsible forestry
FSC™ C020056
FSC
www.fsc.org

ABOUT THE AUTHORS

DARRA GOLDSTEIN the founding editor of *Gastronomica*, is the author of six award-winning cookbooks, including *Beyond the North Wind: Russia in Recipes and Lore,* named one of 2020's best cookbooks by *Forbes.com, Esquire*, and the *Washington Post*. In 2020 she was honored with the Lifetime Achievement Award from the International Association of Culinary Professionals.

CORTNEY BURNS (with chef Nick Balla) built a larder-based kitchen at San Francisco's Bar Tartine; their cookbook *Bar Tartine* won awards from both the James Beard Foundation and IACP. *Bon Appétit* has dubbed her the "godmother of fermentation" for her modern take on ancient techniques.

RICHARD MARTIN is a media executive, lifestyle editor, and writer who started magazines and websites that have grown into major media companies, including *Complex, Modern Luxury* (Manhattan and Miami), and *Food Republic*.